The Effective
Anger Management
Workbook for Parents

Navigating Your Anger for Your Child's Emotional Well-Being With Strategies and Exercises That Positively Impact Your Children's Lives

Richard Bass

© **Copyright 2024 - All rights reserved.**

The content contained within this book may not be reproduced, duplicated or transmitted without direct written permission from the author or the publisher.

Under no circumstances will any blame or legal responsibility be held against the publisher, or author, for any damages, reparation, or monetary loss due to the information contained within this book, either directly or indirectly.

LEGAL NOTICE:

This book is copyright protected. It is only for personal use. You cannot amend, distribute, sell, use, quote or paraphrase any part, or the content within this book, without the consent of the author or publisher.

DISCLAIMER NOTICE:

Please note the information contained within this document is for educational and entertainment purposes only. All effort has been executed to present accurate, up to date, reliable, complete information. No warranties of any kind are declared or implied. Readers acknowledge that the author is not engaged in the rendering of legal, financial, medical or professional advice. The content within this book has been derived from various sources. Please consult a licensed professional before attempting any techniques outlined in this book.

By reading this document, the reader agrees that under no circumstances is the author responsible for any losses, direct or indirect, that are incurred as a result of the use of the information contained within this document, including, but not limited to, errors, omissions, or inaccuracies.

CONTENTS

Introduction — 1.

Chapter 1:
Identify and Manage Emotional Triggers — 4.

Chapter 2:
Master Emotional Intelligence Skills — 20.

Chapter 3:
Stress Management Techniques to Regain Control — 37.

Chapter 4:
Increase Cooperation With Open Communication — 54.

Chapter 5:
Positive Conflict Resolution Skills — 67.

Conclusion:
Take Control of Your Anger, One Day at a Time — 85.

About the Author:
Richard Bass — 86.

References:
Images References — 88.

TRIGGER WARNING:

The contents of this workbook may be harmful to sensitive readers.

INTRODUCTION

Is Anger Bad?

Holding on to anger is like grasping a hot coal with the intent of throwing it at someone else; you are the one who gets burned.
- Buddha

Parenting has its ups and downs. Sometimes, you feel confident and in control of your emotions, and other times, you feel volatile and ready to explode at the slightest mistakes your child makes. What's troubling is that you may not always be able to predict an explosive reaction early enough to calm yourself. By the time you realize how upset you are, the trigger has been activated, and the frightening side of you comes out.

The primary emotion behind your strong reactions is anger-a natural and common emotion to experience. Your anger is a sign that something isn't sitting well with you. Perhaps it is the disrespectful tone of voice your teenage son used when talking to you, your toddler's refusal to listen and follow instructions despite being patient with them, or the lack of help you get from your grown children around the house.

There are many valid reasons why you may react with anger toward your child. Feeling and expressing anger isn't a bad thing; what's concerning is not having control over your anger and making choices that you later regret. The difference between anger that leads to your child's cooperation and anger that emotionally scars them is determined by how much self-awareness and self-regulation you can show.

If you can identify yourself as a parent struggling with anger issues, you have won half of the battle. The fact that you can see the destructive nature of your anger means that you have cultivated a level of self-awareness. The next hurdle you need to overcome is learning how to regulate your anger using effective coping mechanisms whenever you feel like exploding.

Anger Management for Parents

Anger management is a practice that teaches you how to identify and respond to anger constructively. Instead of denying or suppressing the strong emotions you feel, you are taught how to process and release them without harming yourself or others.

Being equipped with anger management skills improves the way you respond to common parenting challenges like handling an uncooperative child or disciplining them in a manner that prevents power struggles. These skills also empower you with the tools to get behind the root of your anger and unlearn harmful behavioral patterns that compromise your relationship with your child.

Perhaps your anger issues date back to childhood when you were frustrated with your parents or living conditions. The inability to regulate your emotions during that time caused you to learn unhealthy ways to handle stress. Those unhealthy coping strategies could be the same ones you use to communicate your disapproval to your child. Unconsciously, you teach them to manage stress in the same way, and your child grows up with similar emotional regulation issues and an unhealthy relationship with anger.

Ending the cycle of poor emotional regulation starts with you as the parent. Through practicing the anger management skills offered in this workbook, you can regain control over your strong emotions and learn various ways to address your child's difficult behaviors using creative and conscious parenting techniques.

How to Use This Workbook

The real problem is not that you get angry with your child sometimes, but the choices you make when you get angry. This workbook has been designed to help you make positive choices on how to manage your anger.

This practical skills-based workbook is accompanied by a full-length theoretical book, written by the same author, titled The Effective Anger Management Guide for Parents: Discover How to Manage and Calm Your Emotions; Turn Your Frustration Into Positive Parenting. The full-length book takes a deep dive into the source of your anger issues and the psychological interventions that can help you positively transform your parenting approach.

The purpose of the workbook is to offer practical at-home anger management exercises that you can use when interacting with your child. The exercises cover several aspects of anger management, such as recognizing and managing emotional triggers, developing emotional intelligence, adopting healthy stress management techniques, improving communication, and cultivating positive conflict resolution skills.

Practicing these exercises is the positive first step you can take to transform your relationship with anger and significantly improve the quality of your relationships. If you are ready to learn healthier ways to manage stress, your master class starts now!

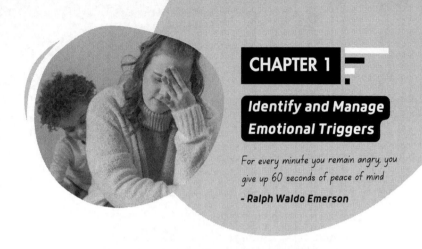

CHAPTER 1

Identify and Manage Emotional Triggers

For every minute you remain angry, you give up 60 seconds of peace of mind
- Ralph Waldo Emerson

Introduction to Emotional Triggers

Stress is a survival response activated when your life is in potential danger. Imagine that your body is a house, and your built-in stress response is the alarm system. Whenever an internal or external crisis occurs, the alarm goes off, and your body is notified to prepare to fight, flee, or freeze. This is how you have survived through the most challenging times.

Your alarm system has always protected you from potential harm and given you a heads-up to prepare for whatever may come. Nevertheless, at some point, the significant amount of stress in your life-whether as a young child or a grown adult-became so overwhelming that your alarm system got jammed. Instead of going off only when your life was in danger, it was triggered by everyday non-threatening experiences.

Emotional triggers are false alarms that go off whenever a current situation reminds you of a difficult crisis or traumatic experience you have been through. Even though there isn't a major threat imposed, your mind behaves as though there is. When feeling triggered, your emotional reactions do not match the gravity of the situation. In many cases, they are extreme, explosive, and not aligned with what's happening right now.

While everybody reacts differently to emotional triggers, here are the common symptoms:

- *feeling unsafe, anxious, or panicked*
- *feeling restless and wanting to escape*
- *increased heart rate and difficulty breathing*
- *overthinking and negative self-talk*
- *unexplainable mood swings*
- *avoidant behaviors like wanting to isolate*
- *flashbacks of past traumatic experiences*
- *emotional outbursts of anger or sadness*
- *feeling impulsive, wanting to say or do inappropriate things*

Since emotional triggers manifest in different ways, the best way to understand how they come about is to learn the cycle. Generally, emotional triggers form in four stages:

Stage 1: Experience: An event or crisis occurs in your life that activates your stress response and generates strong emotions. If it is a traumatic event, your sense of safety is compromised. This impacts the validity of your beliefs and your relationships with others.

Stage 2: Association: Over time, you become hyper-vigilant of any source of stimuli or symbol that reminds you of the painful experience. This is your body's way of protecting you from being blindsided by the same situation in the future. An association can be made with anything, such as smells, sounds, places, words, or people who resemble aspects of the experience.

■ **Stage 3: Memory:** The associations are stored in your long-term memory, making it easier to recognize potential threats from a distance. This explains why emotional triggers often evoke strong emotional reactions that seem unreasonable compared to the situation taking place. Your brain pulls up a memory of the trauma to warn you of potential harm without assessing the risks of your current situation and responding accordingly.

■ **Stage 4: Trigger:** The flashback of the trauma, along with the overwhelming emotions you feel, sets off the trigger. At this stage, you are not reacting to what is happening in front of you but instead reacting to what happened in the past. Your body enters survival mode and seeks to protect you using various coping mechanisms—many of which end up harming you or those around you.

Getting Behind Emotional Triggers

There are different causes of emotional triggers, such as possessing certain personality traits like neuroticism or living with a diagnosed or undiagnosed mental health condition like bipolar disorder or depression. Emotional triggers could also be caused by your genetic makeup or the stressful environment you are exposed to. However, by far, the most common cause of emotional triggers is childhood trauma and the long-term consequences of unhealthy parenting and family dynamics.

Growing up in a family where safety was compromised, or nurturing was shown inconsistently could have been traumatic. Even though your needs as a child were basic, you required a stable, secure, and predictable environment to thrive. A major cause for your emotional triggers could be the physical or emotional neglect you experienced being raised by preoccupied or abusive parents. When you counted on them to show up for you, they were either absent or dismissive of your needs. As a result, you felt unsafe, anxious, angry, and stressed.

Besides the unhealthy family bonds, your emotional triggers could also be rooted in harmful childhood experiences that changed the way you perceive yourself and the world around you. Examples of these experiences include:

- **Childhood trauma:** Being exposed to experiences that cause physical or emotional distress during childhood, such as being orphaned, subjected to abuse, experiencing homelessness, being abandoned by your parents, processing grief, suffering from ongoing sickness, or being a victim of bullying, can create deep wounds. Even years after the trauma occurred, the memories and flashbacks of these experiences could haunt you and interfere with your daily functioning.

- **Childhood fears:** Developing fears and phobias as a child can cause significant stress and anxiety and change the way you think and feel about the world. These fears may be rational (i.e., the fear of an aggressive parent), or they may be irrational (i.e., the fear of embarrassing yourself in public). When these fears are triggered in adulthood, they elicit the same strong emotional reactions experienced as a child.

- **Childhood transitions:** If coping and adapting to change was a difficult process for you as a child, the experience may have left you feeling traumatized. Life transitions like the death of a parent, being separated from your parents, witnessing the divorce of your parents, or adjusting to the financial turmoil and change of lifestyle in your family can create ongoing stress and anxiety as an adult. As a result, you may have low stress tolerance or an irrational fear of change. Life situations that make you feel a lack of control could trigger memories of your unstable past.

If you are interested in learning more about your childhood and the source of your emotional triggers or desire an in-depth analysis of your early childhood wounds, get yourself a copy of the comprehen --

sive anger management book part of this series titled *The Effective Anger Management Guide for Parents: Discover How to Manage and Calm Your Emotions; Turn Your Frustration Into Positive Parenting.*

EXERCISES TO IDENTIFY AND MANAGE EMOTIONAL TRIGGER

You can gain control of your emotional triggers by learning how to identify and manage them properly. The following exercises will show you how to get started.

Exercise 1: Trigger Journaling

Journaling is an effective way to understand and process your emotions without acting on them. The practice of journaling is simple: Grab a pen and a notebook and start writing down whatever comes to your mind.

Trigger journaling focuses particularly on recognizing and understanding how your triggers emerge, what they feel like, what urges they bring up, and the possible causes behind them. In the long run, this practice can help you predict triggering situations and put in place preventative measures to avoid getting upset. Furthermore, you can start to notice patterns of coping behaviors you turn to whenever you are triggered and become more intentional about the choices you make in those vulnerable moments.

Dedicate 10 minutes each day to journaling about the situations that provoked you. To make your entries impactful, ensure your responses are rich with information you can use later to gain a better understanding of your triggers and identify patterns. Don't think too hard about what you write or how it might sound to someone else- nobody will have access to your journal entries unless you give consent.

Forget about spelling and grammar rules and focus on writing what spontaneously comes up in your mind. For more assistance, here are journal prompts to help you start the process:

- What situation made you feel stressed, anxious, or emotional?
- What specific attitudes, words, or behaviors provoked you?
- What thoughts and feelings rushed over your mind and heart?
- What physical sensations did you feel emerge in your body?
- How does this situation compare to previous times when you were provoked?
- What past experiences did this situation remind you of?
- What strong urges did you feel? How did you respond to these urges?
- How did you feel immediately after responding that way?
- What would you change or improve about your response?

Exercise 2: Trigger Mapping

Experiencing emotional triggers is common and shouldn't be considered a bad thing. However, it is important to learn how to recognize them so that you aren't caught off guard when they arise. The ability to anticipate your triggers can also help you plan your responses well in advance and prevent inappropriate or harmful reactions.

Trigger mapping is an effective planning tool that will enable you to get in front of your emotional triggers and have better control over them. Setting up the tools involves charting the characteristics of your triggers on a table, giving you the full picture of what physical, mental, and emotional changes to expect in certain situations.

It is not compulsory to complete your table in one sitting because you may recognize new triggers as time goes by. Alternatively, with time, your response to common triggers may change, and your table entry will need to be adjusted. Therefore, think of trigger mapping as a continuous exercise you practice and modify regularly.

When creating your table, insert five columns and as many rows as you like. The columns should have the following categories:

- **Column 1:** Situation.
- **Column 2:** Physical response.
- **Column 3:** Emotional response.
- **Column 4:** Related behavior.
- **Column 5:** Alternative behavior.

Add the relevant information under each column whenever a new trigger emerges. Note that these can be triggers related to parenting or other areas of your life. The final column, Alternative Behavior, helps you think of practical ways to respond to your triggers when caught in a similar situation in the future. Keep your table in an accessible place so you can refer to it whenever you need to.

Here is an example of a completed row:

Situation	Physical response	Emotional response	Related behavior	Alternative behavior
Toddler crying uncontrollably	• rapid heartbeat • hot flushes • muscle tension	• irritation • panic • anxiety	• yelling • threatening • walking away	• holding child • comforting • validating the child's feelings

Exercise 3: Emotion Identification

It can be easier to identify the physical signs of triggers compared to the emotional ones because sensations are objective (e.g., sweaty palms), whereas emotions are subjective and nuanced. For example, you might notice that you are triggered by a certain situation by the changes to your breathing pattern but fail to pinpoint how the situation makes you feel.

Learning to identify and describe your emotions helps you manage highly stressful situations and gain control of your reactions. The wealth of knowledge that you learn about your emotions strengthens the relationship you have with them. For instance, once you have identified feeling enraged by a specific situation, you can isolate the emotion and look at it through a microscope, analyzing the details of how and when rage surfaces, the beliefs and urges associated with your rage, and how rage relates to your past experiences.

Being knowledgeable about your rage reduces the fear or stress you may feel when it resurfaces and encourages you to think of better ways to express yourself that are not as harmful.

The following table provides a list of unpleasant emotions. Each day, pick an emotion to reflect on and journal about. Write as much as you can about the emotion, and make sure your entry includes the following information:

- *Which situations trigger this emotion?*
- *What beliefs and urges are associated with this emotion?*
- *How does this emotion relate to past experiences?*

fear	stress	anger	shame	guilt	pride
worry	depression	anxiety	rejection	failure	grief
frustration	envy	sadness	loneliness	isolation	disgust
defensive	indifferent	doubtful	confused	desperate	humiliation
disrespected	hateful	withdrawn	betrayed	discouraged	pessimistic

Exercise 4: Role Reversal

A powerful way to learn how to manage your emotional triggers is to start seeing your explosive reactions from your family members' perspective. In psychodrama, this technique is known as role reversal, an effective way to cultivate empathy and gain insights into your behaviors from an outsider's viewpoint.

Role reversal involves switching roles with another family member and allowing yourself to imagine what they think and feel when you are emotionally triggered. While fully immersed and concentrated on their reality, you can reflect on the following questions:

- *How does your body language change immediately before and during a trigger?*
- *How attentive are you to the other person's needs? Do you notice them?*
- *How do you make the other person feel? What emotions do they experience?*
- *How does the other person cope? How do they regulate and protect themselves?*
- *What does the other person think in their mind? What does their inner critic say to them?*

Another way to practice role reversal is to write a letter addressed to you from the other person's perspective. In the letter, describe their experience witnessing or being at the receiving end of your explosive reactions. Explore the emotional impact and long-term consequences of your emotions that you wouldn't otherwise be aware of. Lastly, end the letter by suggesting better ways to handle stressful situations; what requests would the other person make?

Exercise 5: Cognitive Restructuring

Negative thinking patterns can exacerbate feelings of stress and cause you to perceive unpleasant situations as being worse than they are. In this compromised state of mind, you are likely to overreact and do things you otherwise wouldn't do under normal circumstances.

For example, when your child fails to complete their chores for the day, your inner critic might convince you that your child doesn't respect you. As a result, you may end up taking harsh measures that don't match the minor offense of not completing chores. In psychology, these oversights or thinking errors are called cognitive distortions, and they can be corrected through a technique known as cognitive restructuring.

Cognitive restructuring challenges you to perceive reality as it is and not as you assume it to be. Your task when correcting cognitive distortions is to look for factual evidence informing your beliefs and assumptions. When there isn't any factual evidence, you can conclude that the belief or assumption is unreliable and, therefore, should not determine your perception.

There are several ways to challenge your thinking errors. However, the first step is to recognize the negative thoughts, beliefs, or assumptions associated with your emotional triggers. Grab five sheets of paper and fold them into two. With a pair of scissors, cut each sheet of paper in half along the fold line. This should give you ten smaller pieces of paper.

At the top of each paper, write down a common triggering situation and the negative thought, belief, or assumption associated with it, like this:

- **Situation:** My grown children do not show appreciation.
- **Thought:** My children take me for granted.

The next step is to look for factual evidence supporting this thought or conclude that it is unreliable. On the remainder of the page, make a case for or against your cognitive distortion. You can do this by responding honestly to these questions:

- *Is this thought based on facts or opinion?*
- *What factors have you overlooked?*
- *What other ways could this situation be interpreted?*
- *Is this thought black or white, or does it consider the shades of grey?*
- *Would someone else draw the same conclusions that you did?*

Finally, give your verdict on whether or not your thought is reliable. If you discover that it isn't, suggest a fair and balanced perspective that isn't too negative or too positive and one that takes into consideration the information collected.

Exercise 6: Self-Compassion Meditation

Managing emotional triggers can be frustrating. Sometimes, you catch them early enough to prevent a blow-up and other times, you wake up too late and find yourself saying or doing things that harm others. To sustain your continued efforts at controlling your triggers, it is important to practice self-compassion, especially during the low points when you feel discouraged.

Self-compassion is the practice of treating yourself like you would treat a dear friend. When you are overwhelmed and feel like you are carrying the world on your shoulders, self-compassion enables you to be kind and nonjudgmental toward your struggles. The epitome of self-compassion is accepting that you are doing the best you can as a parent and that while there are areas where you can improve, you are proud of the awareness and accountability you have shown in identifying these issues.

Self-compassion meditation is a wonderful way to develop a gentle and loving approach toward your suffering. It teaches you how to open your heart and accept your desirable and undesirable traits without showing favoritism. Moreover, the practice fosters emotional resilience, so you can maintain an optimistic attitude about managing your emotional triggers and anger issues.

Record the following script, then sit down comfortably in a quiet room and play it over for yourself:

Inhale through your nose and exhale out your mouth. Repeat this breathing pattern, slowly and intentionally, five more times. Notice the stillness of your mind and body. Feel your muscles relax and loosen up with each breath.

When you are ready, bring to your mind a situation with your child that is causing you stress. For now, choose a mild situation that won't evoke intense emotions. When you become proficient in this exercise, you can focus on bigger problems. Replay how the situation started and how it has progressed over time. Think about the things that grieve you the most about the situation.

Connect to how you feel and spend a few minutes sitting with your emotions. Observe them without judging their appropriateness. Practice saying the following statements to yourself in light of how you are feeling at the moment:

- *This feeling hurts.*
- *I am not the only parent who feels this way.*
- *May I be gentle with myself.*

Repeat the statements a few times, each time noticing how they affect your mind and body. Do you feel less heaviness? Does the situation seem manageable? You are welcome to customize the statements to feel more authentic to how you would comfort yourself. At the end of the session, journal about your experience.

Exercise 7: Trigger Prevention Plan

Everybody copes and reacts differently to stress. However, in the absence of healthy coping strategies, you run the risk of making choices that are not in your best interests. Emotional triggers can be prevented by improving your response to stress and learning to act on the early warning signs before they develop into bigger symptoms.

The early warning signs to look out for include:

- *trouble sleeping (i.e., sleeping too much or too little)*
- *changes in your appetite (i.e., eating too much or too little)*
- *hypersensitivity to sounds, smells, lights, food, etc.*
- *regular migraines and heaviness*
- *chronic fatigue and lethargy*
- *isolation or withdrawal from others*
- *frequent mood swings and emotional outbursts*
- *difficulty concentrating or staying motivated*

Compiling a trigger prevention plan helps you prepare for parenting challenges that may cause stress and anxiety. This works best when there is a future situation you are feeling anxious about and can start mentally preparing yourself for. For example, you might prepare for a boundaries conversation with your child, which could get heated, or a co-parenting discussion with the mother or father of your child, which has the potential to trigger you.

Your plan must be broken down into three phases, highlighting positive coping strategies to practice before, during, and after the situation has occurred. If you want a more detailed plan, you can think of strategies to practice months, weeks, and days in advance. The aim is to provide yourself with enough positive reinforcement to curb emotional triggers. Note that this plan works best when you are aware of the potential triggers and how you normally behave in those stressful situations. This gives you enough information to carefully select alternative behaviors that will work for you.

Here is a table with healthy coping strategies to get you started. You are free to research other meaningful practices to incorporate into your trigger prevention plan.

deep breathing	journaling exercises	cognitive restructuring	positive affirmations	eating a healthy diet	improving sleep routine
talking to a therapist	joining a support group	asking for help	physical exercise	reading a self-help book	rehearsing setting boundaries
practicing acceptance	abstaining from drugs and alcohol	getting a relaxing massage	going for a walk or hike	taking time off work	coloring in or doodling
organizing your life, using lists and calendars	practicing gratitude	catching up with friends and family	saying heartfelt prayers	practicing meditation	learning new coping skills
listening to motivational podcasts	practicing visualization	taking a nap	decluttering your house	writing a letter to your future self	encouraging someone else

Exercise 8: Seeking Professional Support

It takes strength to admit that you cannot control your intense and frequent emotional outbursts on your own. If you ever reach this point, rest assured that professional support is available.

Only you will know when professional assistance is required. Some of the signs might be developing abusive patterns, turning to substances to self-medicate, a weakened immune system that causes you to get sick often, or feeling disconnected from yourself and others.

Please note that you don't necessarily have to wait until you incur severe physical, social, or psychological problems to seek help. Doctors can create a custom treatment plan to respond to the symptoms you are experiencing. They can also diagnose underlying mental health conditions-if any-and recommend relevant forms of therapy to teach you healthy coping strategies.

Speak to your family doctor or consult a psychotherapist to get started on your recovery plan. Schedule appointments with at least three doctors and get to know their approach to treating anger issues. It is important to choose a doctor whom you trust and resonate with because the process of healing anger issues requires vulnerability and commitment.

On the day of your first consultations, ask your doctors a series of interview questions similar to these:

- *How did you get into this profession?*
- *How long have you been practicing?*
- *How long have you been treating clients with anger issues?*
- *What positive results have you seen from your clients?*
- *Which professional associations are you a member of?*
- *What certifications and qualifications do you have?*
- *What is your unique approach to counseling?*
- *How are sessions structured? Is there homework given?*
- *What forms of therapy do you administer? What are the benefits?*
- *How often would you recommend seeing me? How long is each session?*

Combating emotional triggers is the first step to managing your anger. Once you are comfortable identifying and controlling your emotions, you can begin to cultivate emotional intelligence. The next chapter will show you how!

CHAPTER 2

Master Emotional Intelligence Skills

You can't selectively numb your anger any more than you can turn off all lights in a room and still expect to see the light.
- **Shannon L. Alder**

Introduction to Emotional Intelligence

According to Mental Health America (2023), emotional intelligence (EQ) is defined as "the ability to both manage your own emotions and understand the emotions of people around you." To do this, it is important to learn how to recognize what and how you are feeling and use that intelligence to empathize with what and how others might be feeling. In other words, developing EQ begins by improving your self-awareness and emotional regulation skills.

The purpose of EQ is to understand your thoughts, feelings, and behaviors and how they impact your relationships. It allows you to take a step back and observe how you make others feel, the effectiveness of your communication, the decisions you make that can affect others, and the various ways you respond to stress and conflict. With that said, there are limitations to practicing EQ, such as you cannot manage or change another person's thoughts, feelings, or behaviors. The most you can do is understand what they may be thinking or feeling and how those thoughts or emotions impact their behaviors and worldview.

There are many benefits to developing EQ as a parent. First and foremost, it teaches you to focus on understanding your child and what they need from you. When you identify and empathize with what your child needs, you can modify your behaviors accordingly, thereby strengthening your relationship. Second, EQ teaches you that your perspective is only one side of the story and that other perspectives can give you a wider and richer outlook on your situation. It encourages you to be more open and willing to embrace the ideas, opinions, and beliefs of others, to find common ground during conflict, and to see differences as opportunities to learn and connect.

Lastly, having EQ radically transforms your parenting style. In an article, psychologist Dr. John Gottman identifies two types of parents and how they handle emotions (Gottman, 2018). The first type is emotion-dismissing parents who feel uncomfortable processing or watching their children be emotional. They see emotionality as potentially destructive for them and their children's ability to get things done.

The second type is emotion-coaching parents who accept and hold space for their children to feel and express their emotions. They are also attuned to their own emotions, which makes it easier to coach their children on how to manage theirs. Research conducted by the John Gottman Institute found that children from emotion-coaching parents were more emotionally stable and resilient and coped better with life transitions like divorce or increasing demands from school (Hooven et al., 1995).

Four Emotional Intelligence Skills

As a parent, you are emotionally invested in the well-being of your child. However, beyond desiring the best outcomes for them, it is important to understand how your behaviors and parenting approach impact their well-being. EQ is multifaceted and revolves around four core skills: self-awareness, self-regulation, social awareness, and relationship management. These skills play a crucial role in cultivating emotional maturity and nurturing your parent-child relationship.

Here is a brief overview of the four EQ skills:

Self-Awareness

Self-awareness refers to the ability to recognize your thoughts and emotions. It requires a level of introspection, where you demonstrate curiosity about what you think and feel, how and when these experiences come about, and why you carry certain perceptions or feelings about situations or people. Being a self-aware parent means that you can identify and describe your thoughts and feelings and make a connection between the events that take place in your mind and those that take place in your household.

Self-Regulation

Self-regulation, also known as self-management, refers to the ability to control your emotional and behavioral responses. This skill becomes increasingly important when you are feeling stressed or overwhelmed and run a higher risk of being emotionally triggered by situations. Improving your self-regulation skills requires you to learn how to delay your reactions through a powerful pause and reflect on the best choices you can make in every unique circumstance. Moreover, you are encouraged to take accountability for your poor choices in behaviors and seek to modify them by adopting positive habits.

Social Awareness

Social awareness takes an outside-in approach to assessing and modifying your behaviors. It involves reflecting on how you positively or negatively impact other people and learning to become more conscious and empathetic to the needs of others. Practicing social awareness can make you a better communicator and negotiator with your child. It teaches you how to accept diverse perspectives and experiences, which enables you to create a safe space for your child to share their thoughts and feelings openly and resolve conflict without compromising the trust and openness in your parent-child relationship.

Relationship Management

Relationship management refers to the ability to build and maintain healthy and nurturing relationships. For this to happen, there are several interpersonal skills that you need to learn, including mindful communication, active listening, positive conflict resolution, boundary setting, and positive reinforcement. As your child grows, their needs and expectations from you will change. Relationship management allows you to adapt your responses and approaches to parenting to maintain a healthy relationship with your child.

EXERCISES TO MASTER EMOTIONAL INTELLIGENCE SKILLS

You can become more comfortable with your emotions and express them in healthy ways without harming your child or family members. The following exercises reinforce the four skills outlined above and provide enough practice material to master emotional intelligence.

Exercise 9: Anger Thermometer

An anger thermometer is a visual aid best used at home to label and describe the intensity of anger you are feeling. It can be helpful when you have a small child who isn't yet proficient in the use of language or for an older child who prefers short and impactful communication over long explanations about how you are feeling.

Furthermore, if you are not yet confident or comfortable with expressing your feelings, the anger thermometer communicates your emotions on your behalf. You simply need to refer to specific points or zones on the thermometer to notify your child about your feelings. Creating an anger thermometer is simple. You will need a large piece of cardboard paper and some craft materials, then follow these instructions:

1. Start by outlining the shape of a temperature thermometer on the page with an erasable pencil. Leave enough space on both sides of the thermometer to add some text later on.

2. Still using an erasable pencil, create a 10-point scale inside the thermometer. You can choose how to design the scale; for example, you can count in single digits from 1-10 or count in multiples of 2 (i.e., 2, 4, 6, 8, 10).

3. Once you are comfortable with the design of your thermometer, go over all the pencil lines with a chunky and thin black marker- the chunky marker is used for the outline of the thermometer and the think marker for the 10-point scale.

4. Grab four coloring pencils: green, yellow, orange, and red. Section your thermometer into four zones and color each zone with the corresponding coloring pencil. The circular tip of the thermometer is the green zone, followed by the yellow, orange, and red zone.

5. Label each zone with a name that describes your intensity of anger at each stage. For example, the green zone could be "calm," the yellow zone could be "moody," the orange zone could be "angry," and the red zone could be "furious."

5 On the left side of the thermometer, put the heading "What does it feel like?" On the right side of the thermometer, put the heading "What helps?" On the left side of each zone, describe what you are feeling using keywords, then on the right, describe what helps you regulate your emotions—the green zone can be left blank on this side.

Now, your anger thermometer is complete. Introduce the chart to your child and family members and explain when and how it will be used. Educate them on terms you will use to refer to how you are feeling. For example, when you say, "I'm in the yellow zone right now. Can I have 10 minutes to breathe?" your child should know what emotion you are referring to and how your request is a type of coping strategy.

Exercise 10: Using "I" Statement Requests

EQ compels you to become mindful of the impact and intent behind your words. You might have good intentions to drive across a specific message, but due to not phrasing your message correctly, the main idea gets lost in translation and may even upset the listener.

"I" statement requests are specific phrases you can use when expressing your concerns to your child. They revolve around taking responsibility for your emotions, describing the impact of the concerning behavior, and asking for what you need. Your message becomes about you and less focused on the other person. Using this structure allows the listener to lower their defenses and listen to what you have to say without feeling attacked. Furthermore, it shows you how to express strong emotions in a controlled way and make requests respectfully.

There are five phrases to use, in the order they are presented below when making "I" statement requests (Astray, 2020):

1. *When you... [describe concerning behavior]*
2. *I feel... [name the emotions]*
3. *The story I'm telling myself is... [state the assumption made]*
4. *I need... [make a direct and clear request]*
5. *Would you... [suggest an appropriate action or behavior]*

> **Here is an example of a completed request:**
> *"When you make rude comments to me, I feel angry and disappointed. The story I'm telling myself is that you don't care about me as your father. I need you to show me more respect. Would you please watch your language when speaking to me?"*

Think of real-life scenarios when you would use this formula and practice making requests, adding your personal touch!

Exercise 11: Take the Opposite Action

The oldest and most primitive part of your brain, which consists of your amygdala, brain stem, and limbic region, controls your survival responses like breathing, heart function, digestion, and reacting to perceived danger. When you are stressed, this area lights up, and you begin to experience the physiological signs of stress. At that stage, your body is prepared to defend itself from possible harm by all means necessary.

Being reactive to stress can make situations worse rather than better. EQ teaches you how to identify the sensations of stress but choose alternative ways to respond to them. Instead of acting upon your biological instincts, you are encouraged to activate a different part of your brain-the prefrontal cortex-which is responsible for executive planning and problem-solving.

A technique that can help you make this shift is known as opposite action. It is a dialectical behavioral therapy (DBT) skill that promotes self-regulation and can increase your stress tolerance. As the name suggests, taking the opposite action is about doing what is right, not what feels good. To know what is the right action to take in any situation, you need to delay your response and take a few minutes to calm your mind and think about your desired outcome.

For example, when you are angry with your child for not cleaning up after themself, what feels good is yelling at them and letting out the enormous energy trapped inside of you. However, if your desired outcome is to increase cooperation and motivate them to adopt different habits, yelling is not the right thing to do. In this case, the right thing would be to sit them down and understand what factors could be contributing to their reluctance and how you can support them in instilling positive habits (e.g., creating a weekly timetable of chores they must complete).

The following table provides you with common upsetting behaviors your child might display. For each scenario, think about and write down what responses would feel good (i.e., give you a sense of relief or pleasure), the desired outcomes, and what responses would be the right thing to do (i.e., taking the opposite action aligned with the desired outcomes).

Situation	What feels good?	What is the desired outcome?	What is the right thing to do?
Back-talking			
Lack of gratitude			
Uncleanliness			
Silent treatment			
Rebellion			
Lying			

Arrogance			
Not listening			
No accountability			
Saying hurtful words			

Exercise 12: Build Your Self-Care Routine

Regularly practicing self-care is an effective way to take care of your survival and emotional needs so you can prevent burnout, emotional triggers, and unhealthy coping mechanisms. Instead of seeing self-care as an indulgent activity that you don't have time for, choose to see it instead as a preventative plan to avoid mental and emotional issues.

Remember that before you can focus on your child's well-being, you need to prioritize your well-being. Self-care doesn't need to cost you a ton of money or take up a lot of your time. It simply needs to be relevant to your needs and yield positive results. The following tips will help you build a meaningful self-care routine catered to your needs and lifestyle:

- **Set intentions and goals for your self-care:** Think about what you hope to achieve by incorporating self-care into your daily life. In what ways do you want the routine to support your needs? How do you want to feel after practicing the routine?

- **Choose realistic and effective practices:** Identify meaningful practices that can respond to your needs. For example, if you need more rest, put yourself on a bedtime schedule. If you need to socialize more, stay in touch with friends and family. Your practices must focus on improving your wellness and countering symptoms of stress.

- **Schedule time for self-care in your calendar:** To avoid forgetting about prioritizing your needs, carve out time to practice self-care. Find gaps in between your busy day-even five-minute slots are doable-to complete your practices. During that time, put your phone on silent, close your laptop, and be present in the moment.

- **Seek support from your community:** Share your self-care intentions and goals with your community and seek support and encouragement. Be forthcoming about how they can assist you on this journey. For example, if you have a yoga appointment and need to organize someone else to pick up your child from school, make those arrangements well in advance.

Exercise 13: Empathy Map

In an argument, there are always three sides to the story: the first person's defense, the second person's defense, and the unbiased truth. In most cases, parents hold onto their defense, and so do their children, which makes it difficult for both parties to understand each other and work toward arriving at the truth together.

An empathy map is a visual tool that allows you to understand your attitudes and behaviors on a deeper level, as well as the motivations behind your child's attitudes and behaviors. It consists of four quadrants that explore what you say, think, do, and feel during specific situations. You can create an empathy map whenever you seek to gain more insight into the source and triggers of a conflict between you and your child.

Start by creating a map for yourself, then create a map from the perspective of your child. Feel free to sit down with them and discuss both maps and help each other see the motivations behind your actions.

A completed empathy map for you will look similar to this:

What I say...	What I think...
<ul><li>You don't listen</li><li>What are you thinking?</li><li>Why are you so stubborn?</li></ul>	<ul><li>She is testing my patience</li><li>Am I not doing enough as a parent?</li><li>I have to show them who's the boss</li></ul>

What I do...	What I feel...
• Take away privileges • Limit communication with my child • Give them more rules and expectations to follow	• challenged • disrespected • lack of support • overwhelmed

Your child's empathy map may look like this:

What she says...	What she thinks...
• You don't care about me • Respect goes both ways • Why do you keep shouting at me?	• My mother is controlling • Nobody understands me • I am always the bad person
What she does...	**What she feels...**
• Take away privileges • Limit communication with my child • Give them more rules and expectations to follow	• judged • disrespected • lack of support • overwhelmed

After completing both empathy maps, look for similarities between what you and your child think and feel. It is common to find overlaps, such as common feelings or behaviors. This shows that your needs aren't as conflicting as you would imagine. You may want the same things but choose different approaches to get them.

Exercise 14: Family Emotions Chart

One of the ways to nurture your parent-child relationship is to have frequent conversations about your feelings in a low-stress environment. This ensures that problems are brought up as they arise and resolved quickly to prevent big reactions.

The family emotions chart is another visual aid that illustrates an assortment of emotions. These emotions can be depicted as facial expressions or a collage of words or organized in a table.

Whenever you have an opportunity to spend quality time with your child, bring the emotions chart with you. Ask them to review the chart and indicate what they are feeling at that moment or how they felt during a stressful situation that occurred in the past few days.

Use this as a springboard to listen and validate their emotions, saying phrases like:

- *That makes sense.*
- *I hear you.*
- *I can imagine how stressful that was.*
- *I know what you mean.*

When it is your turn, follow the same instructions and identify an emotion you feel at the moment or over the past few days. Describe your emotional experience using analogies and language that your child will understand. If there are some useful coping strategies that you are practicing, let them know how they have helped you.

Exercise 15: Celebrate Achievements

Positive reinforcement is the practice of paying attention to and rewarding desirable behaviors. This approach to parenting, in particular discipline, motivates your child to modify their behaviors on their own and feel empowered while doing so.

An example of positive reinforcement is celebrating your child's achievements, no matter how big or small. For example, an achievement could be completing homework every day without being reminded for a full week or winning a prize at a competition.

Achievements signal that there is something that your child is doing well. Praising them for their good behavior provides an incentive to continue behaving in this manner. Furthermore, the hyperfocus on good behaviors indirectly discourages them from adopting bad behaviors.

When celebrating your child's achievements, ensure the rewards match the significance of the behaviors they have performed. Save the big rewards for large milestones and use smaller rewards to acknowledge daily, weekly, or monthly progress.

Here are some suggestions of rewards to consider:

- *Praise your child with words.*
- *Buy a small token of appreciation.*
- *Use a stickers or rewards chart.*
- *Take your child on a date.*
- *Cook or buy their favorite meal.*
- *Call extended family members and share the news.*
- *Place their awards and certificates somewhere in the house for others to see.*
- *Create a family rewards tradition-something you do as a family whenever one of you accomplishes something.*

Exercise 16: Parent Time-Out

In positive parenting, we discourage parents from placing their children in a time-out. However, when parents are overwhelmed and feel like exploding on their children, we recommend that they put themselves in a time-out.

Parent time-out involves checking out for five minutes or more and using the time to calm down and recenter yourself. It can look like retreating to your bedroom and practicing breathing exercises to self-soothe, or leaving the house for an hour and running errands or practicing self-care.

The best time to take a parent time-out is when you notice the early signs of stress. Take this as your cue to take a break. Set a timer for a few minutes or an hour, and return to your parenting duties afterward.

If you are going to leave the house, notify your family about where you are going and when you will return. If you have chosen to retreat to your bedroom, put a hanging sign on the door to indicate that you are on a time-out and should not be disturbed. Make sure you leave the time-out feeling calm, refreshed, and in control. There should be a noticeable shift in your mood and a positive difference in your interactions with family members.

Developing EQ is a life skill that can transform your parent-child relationship and improve the way you approach conflict and communication. It can also teach you how to master your emotions and prevent explosive outbursts. In the next chapter, we will look at various stress management techniques you can practice along with EQ skills.

CHAPTER 3

Stress Management Techniques to Regain Control

Don't allow little things to annoy you. At best, you are poisoning your soul. At worst, you are poisoning everyone around you
— **Wayne Gerard Trotman**

Introduction to Stress Management

Parenting can be a stressful job, particularly when you are juggling other responsibilities in your life. What adds to this stress is that your parent-child relationship is constantly evolving as your child's needs, attitudes, and behaviors change. While it is normal to feel overwhelmed by your parenting duties when they get too much, how you choose to manage your stress impacts your overall well-being and the quality of your relationship with your child.

A certain amount of stress can be good for you. This type of stress is called eustress, and it improves your focus, makes you more detail-oriented, and can enhance your performance. Eustress is experienced for short periods before attempting a new task or when pursuing your goals. You may notice the standard symptoms of stress; however, they are manageable.

Stress becomes harmful when not managed properly. It shifts from eustress to a destructive state known as distress. When you are distressed, your stress level hurts your mind and body. It interferes with your ability to think logically, solve problems, and make healthy choices for yourself and your child. Moreover, distress alters your moods and weakens your emotional regulation. Thus, you notice spontaneous feelings of irritability, anger, or overwhelm that come over you at different times of the day.

To reverse the signs and symptoms of distress, it is crucial to incorporate stress management strategies into your daily life. Stress management can be defined as "the set of tools, skills, and strategies that help you reduce stress and improve your physical, mental, and emotional well-being." When stress management is practiced regularly, it serves as a preventative measure to combat stress and maintain good health through the ups and downs of life.

The benefits of stress management for parents are endless. Stress management strategies are designed to fight against mental and physical illness and ensure that you are functioning at your optimal performance as a parent. The strategies address your unmet needs and ongoing crises that cause suffering in your life, which means that you have more energy, creativity, and motivation to dedicate to parenting your child.

Signs That You Are Overwhelmed

If you want to measure how stressed you are, you can use the stress scale. The scale rates your symptoms from 1-10 and determines whether you fall in the low-stress or high-stress range.

Use the scale below to evaluate how stressed you are:

Low-stress zone	Scale
I am content with my life.	1-2
I am in control of my moods.	2-3
I can manage day-to-day stress.	3-5

High-stress zone	Scale
I am moderately irritable or anxious.	5-6
I struggle to manage my day-to-day stress.	6-7
I feel a lack of control in my life.	7-8
I need professional help to treat burnout.	9-10

From point five going upward, you enter the high-stress zone and become vulnerable to stress-related conditions and disorders like parent burnout. This fairly new phenomenon became popular during the COVID-19 pandemic when parents were openly sharing their frustrations related to job insecurity, economic instability, homeschooling, and parenting children with health conditions.

Parent burnout is more than chronic stress. It eventually leads to a complete system shutdown. Early signs of parent burnout are fatigue, migraines, loss of appetite, sleep disturbances, and other common physiological signs of distress. However, over time, it negatively affects your psychological state and causes emotional exhaustion and distancing that can show up as a lack of interest in daily tasks and feeling disconnected from your parental role and relationships with family members. Another way to describe parent burnout is feeling trapped in a lifeless body.

A 2022 study found that 66% of parents report suffering from parent burnout (Gawlik & Melnyk, 2022). While many are working mothers, fathers feel the strain of parenting, too. Single parents and parents raising children with disabilities were seen to be at a higher risk of burnout due to the increased pressure they may feel. The high level of stress combined with the absence of support and resources is a recipe that leads many parents to burnout.

Practicing healthy stress management strategies can be an effective way to prevent parent burnout and prioritize self-care. However, when stress levels become extreme, the best route is to seek professional support from a mental health specialist. If community support is something you lack, consider joining a parenting support group or contributing to parenting forums. When you share your parenting struggles with others, you realize that your symptoms are common and you are not the only mother or father struggling to cope.

EXERCISES TO IMPROVE STRESS MANAGEMENT

You have the strength to beat parent burnout and learn healthier ways to manage stress and the pressures that come with parenting. The following stress management exercises will help you get started.

Exercise 17: Deep Breathing

There is a connection between your breathing and emotions. When your heartbeat accelerates, and you start losing control of the pace and rhythm of your breathing, your body's stress response is triggered, and you may find it difficult to manage strong emotions that arise, like fear, anger, and anxiety. However, when your breathing slows down, you can regulate your body's nervous system and reduce stress symptoms. Taking slow and deep breaths induces relaxation and triggers your brain to release feel-good chemicals known as endorphins. This explains why after a few deep breaths, you feel a sense of relief from emotional distress.

Deep breathing exercises are simple sequences that help regulate your breathing and relieve physical and emotional tension. The following exercises can be carried out anywhere and won't take up much of your time. Repeat each exercise for five cycles for best results.

- **Mindful breathing:** Be aware of your breathing pace, depth, and rhythm without trying to change them. Follow each inhalation and exhalation, each time noticing something new. You can also pay attention to the thoughts and emotions that spontaneously appear in your mind as you are breathing.

- **Box breathing:** Regulate your breathing by making each inhalation and exhalation the same length and depth. Draw an imaginary box by practicing the inhale-hold-exhale-hold sequence for 5-5-5-5 counts. Increase or decrease the counts according to what feels comfortable for you.

- **Nostril breathing:** Close the left nostril with your right index finger and inhale through your right nostril. Hold your breath and switch positions, opening your left nostril and closing your right nostril with your right thumb. Exhale through your left nostril.

Exercise 18: Mindfulness Meditation

Mindfulness meditation is a type of meditative practice that invites you to observe the thoughts, emotions, or sensations that are emerging without attaching yourself to them. For example, if you notice feeling upset, pay attention to how the emotion moves and grows inside of you until it naturally subsides. The practice begins like any traditional meditation, but instead of clearing your mind, you are encouraged to observe, acknowledge, and release incoming stimuli-in that order.

Note that you will feel tempted to judge or draw quick conclusions about some of the stimuli you notice. Nevertheless, challenge yourself to maintain an open and receptive mind. For example, if you feel sadness, do not criticize yourself for feeling this way. Be curious about your sadness, where it comes from, and what you can learn from it. You might even offer words of compassion to yourself and say "It is okay to feel sad. I embrace this feeling."

Another challenging step might be the last one: letting go of what you think, feel, or sense. When you attach yourself to every idea, belief, emotion, or memory that comes to your mind, you can feel distressed and disconnected from reality. Practicing letting go by shifting your focus to something else (i.e., this could be another thought or emotion surfacing). Alternatively, you can imagine that your awareness is the infinite blue sky, and your thoughts or emotions are passing clouds. Your awareness is constant and unchanging; the clouds come in and out of your awareness.

Exercise 19: Time Management Hacks

A common source of stress for parents is the challenge of balancing parenting duties with work life, family responsibilities, household management, and making time for self-care. Time management is a tool that helps you find time to do the important things, as well as the things you love. It can reduce stress related to your work and family commitments and get you close enough to the ideal work-life balance. Time management teaches you how to optimize the 24 hours of the day and get the most value. This is done through hacks or strategies that show you how to plan your day.

Here are some time management hacks to incorporate in your planning:

- **Get your priorities in order:** Not everything you have planned for the day is urgent or important. Some things may seem so, but upon close inspection, you may find they are tasks you can delegate or postpone to a later date. Get your priorities in order by finding the 20% of tasks that bring 80% value-this is also known as Pareto's 80/20 rule. This means if you had 10 tasks, completing 2 of them would make your day successful.

- **Create structured routines:** Having different sets of routines that you carry out during the day ensures you prioritize tasks that bring the highest value. Your routines can be designed around the parts of the day (e.g., morning, afternoon, evening routine, etc.), or they can focus on executing specific tasks well (e.g., work routine, homework routine, dinner prep and cooking routine, etc.).

- **Leverage technology:** Automate recurring manual tasks that take up a lot of time, like paying household bills, shopping for groceries online, responding to emails, budgeting and financial management, assisting your child with homework assignments, or using kitchen cooking gadgets to reduce time spent cooking.

- **Delegate tasks and seek support:** You don't need to carry the responsibility of parenting alone. Create a list of your daily tasks and identify some that you can delegate to your spouse or family members. For example, the whole family might collaborate on doing household chores and cooking meals, and you and your spouse might take turns caring for small children while the other enjoys a night out with their friends. If you have the financial means, consider hiring house help and babysitters to assist with parenting and household tasks.

To hold yourself accountable for managing your time more efficiently, use the following table to track your time and the kind of tasks you spend it on:

Task	Estimated time	Actual time	Frequency	Important
				YES/NO
				YES/NO
				YES/NO

					YES/NO
					YES/NO
					YES/NO
					YES/NO
					YES/NO
					YES/NO
					YES/NO

Exercise 20: Set Clear Expectations With Your Child

You may feel frustrated whenever your child doesn't listen to and follow your instructions. This could be due to a power struggle-particularly with an older child-or poor listening skills related to a learning or behavioral condition. In stressful situations like these, you might tell yourself that your child is testing your limits and challenging your authority. This may or may not be true; however, entertaining this type of thought can emotionally trigger you and lead to an explosive reaction.

Setting clear expectations helps your child learn the difference between acceptable and unacceptable behaviors and provides simple suggestions for them to improve their behaviors moving forward. Clear expectations also come with clear consequences that will follow if your child doesn't follow the right course of action. This means that even if your child doesn't learn from the clear instructions, they will learn by facing appropriate consequences.

Here are some steps on how to set clear expectations with your child:

1 **Be specific:** Be very specific about what you dislike or need. Avoid vague statements like, "That's not good" or "Please listen." Identify the troublesome behavior you would like modified or the desired behavior you expect. **Example:**

- **A** *Younger child:* "I don't like it when you yell in the house when I am working in the study room."

- **B** *Older child:* "When you finish eating your meal, I expect you to put your plate in the kitchen."

2 **Provide an explanation:** Provide age-appropriate explanations that focus on how your child can benefit. Making explanations about them creates a greater incentive for them to willingly follow your instructions. **Example:**

- **A** *Younger child:* "My work moves a lot slower when you are yelling in the house, which means you have to wait longer for us to play together."

- **B** *Older child:* "Cleaning up after yourself prepares you for life when you go to university or start working."

3 **Focus on desired behaviors:** Instead of telling your child what they shouldn't do, show them what good behavior looks like. Be direct when requesting desired behaviors. It should sound like a gentle command rather than a question. **Example:**

- **A** *Younger child:* "Please use your soft voice when playing in the house."

- **B** *Older child:* "I need you to practice getting up and putting your plate away as soon as you finish your meal."

④ Set clear consequences: Consequences, although unpleasant, can be an incentive for your child to listen and follow instructions. The consequences you enforce should match the offense and teach your child something positive. Use the simple "If... then" sentence structure to communicate consequences. **Example:**

- **Ⓐ** *Younger child:* "If you continue yelling in the house while I am working, then you will need to play outside during my work hours."

- **Ⓑ** *Older child:* "If you continue to leave your empty plates around the house, then you will only be allowed to eat your meals in the kitchen."

Go through the four steps using real-life challenges you experience at home. Remember to adjust the language you use to match your child's age and level of understanding.

Exercise 21: Practice Gratitude

It is so easy to get caught up with the duties of parenting that you miss the opportunity to connect with your child. One of the ways to cultivate a close bond with your child and see them in a positive light, even when they misbehave, is to practice grateful parenting. Grateful parenting is "the practice of noticing and appreciating the desirable traits and behaviors of your child" (Dunlea, n.d.). It involves acknowledging their inherent value that exists independently from how they choose to behave.

You can learn grateful parenting by making gratitude a daily practice in your parent-child relationship. Here are some suggestions:

- *Say "Thank you" when your child follows instructions.*
- *Notice positive behaviors and take a few minutes to acknow-*

ledge them.
- Reflect on the progress your child is making in different areas of their life.
- Respect your child's boundaries. Listen when they say "no."
- Tell your child what you love about their personality or choices.

To progressively shift your mindset, document every instance you catch your child behaving well or displaying their talents and strengths and reflect on your list regularly. The following table will help you get started:

What positive actions did your child take?	What is the significance?	How did the actions make you feel?	What did the actions reveal about your child as a person?

Exercise 22: Connect With Others

Stressed and overburdened parents run the risk of socially isolating themselves to cope with emotional distress. However, withdrawing from friends and family can make symptoms of stress worse and promote unhealthy habits. How you socialize now may be different from how you socialized before having a child, so take a moment to figure out what being social means to you and what type of support you need. Three types of support can alleviate stress and anxiety:

- **Informational support:** Seeking knowledge, answers, or advice on how to solve parenting problems or improve your parent-child relationship. This type of support helps to identify key issues and learn how to overcome them.

- **Practical support:** Receiving actionable steps or blueprints on how to effect change and see desired results. This type of support is proactive and based on trial and error. It involves taking informational support and creating plans and strategies to implement change.

- **Emotional support:** Looking for safe spaces or people whom you can share your thoughts and feelings with. The aim is to vent your frustration and offload what is on your mind and heart. Emotional support does not come with solutions on how to address problems unless it is combined with another type of support.

Once you have identified the type of support you need, you can approach the right people to support you. There are direct and indirect sources of support, such as one-on-one interactions with others or going onto websites and joining virtual communities.

Moreover, support can be personal or professional. Personal support involves reaching out to friends and family, and professional support involves speaking to mental health specialists, child doctors, and school teachers.

Reflect on the type of support you need and what that might look like in your life. Identify and write down a list of people who can offer you this support. Reach out to them and be specific about how they can help.

Exercise 23: Engage in Hobbies

Making time for yourself outside your parenting role improves your physical and mental health. One of the ways to do this is by adopting hobbies that provide a positive distraction from parenting responsibilities and promote personal development. Your chosen hobbies can form part of your holistic self-care routine. For instance, you can select hobbies that relieve stress, help you stay physically active, and give you opportunities to get outside and socialize.

The best way to find hobbies you enjoy is to expose yourself to as many activities as possible. Here is a *30-day hobbies challenge* that will encourage you to venture outside your comfort zone and have fun trying new experiences.

Day #	Activity
1	Plant flowers or vegetable seeds.
2	Sign up for an online course.
3	Find a motivational podcast.
4	Discover a new musician.

5	Complete a workout video.
6	Try out a new restaurant.
7	Visit an art gallery.
8	Go to a cooking class.
9	Journal about your day.
10	Take on a small DIY project.
11	Find an expert online who can teach you a new skill.
12	Learn how to knit or sew.
13	Do an adventurous outdoor activity (e.g., hiking, quad biking, water sports, etc.)
14	Listen to live music.
15	Color a picture using a coloring book.
16	Attend a seminar or workshop.
17	Take interesting photos throughout the day and edit them using a photo-editing tool.
18	Drop off supplies at a local shelter.
19	Show support for a social cause.
20	Take a dance class.

21	Redecorate a room in your house.
22	Declutter your house.
23	Consume a healthy and balanced diet.
24	Find a financial advisor and set up a meeting.
25	Download an investment app.
26	Buy a book on a subject you are interested in.
27	Join an online forum based on a challenge you are currently facing.
28	Learn a new language.
29	Create a vision board.
30	Plan a vacation, including the itinerary and budget.

Exercise 24: Create a Stress-Free Morning Routine

If the mornings are chaotic in your household, you can reduce stress by getting your family to follow a fun and productive morning routine. This is simply a schedule that is followed every morning in the same manner. The schedule is supposed to improve your time management and ensure the most important tasks are carried out by your family. You can create a morning routine that is the same for every family member or a routine for each individual. Note that individual routines will require testing, patience, and a lot of encouragement to get implemented.

Here are some tips for creating a stress-free morning routine:

- Make sure everyone gets to bed on time.
- Create charts to help everyone understand their morning routines.
- Create a rewards system to incentivize following morning routines.
- Time how long each task takes and modify your routines accordingly.
- Continuously test to see what works and what doesn't about the routines.
- Get your family members' input about which tasks to include in their morning routines.
- Complete as many of the time-consuming morning tasks like packing school bags, preparing lunch meals, or setting aside an outfit the evening before.

Use the following morning routine planner to start organizing your weekday mornings:

Time	Morning tasks	Mon	Tues	Wed	Thurs	Fri

Managing your stress and anxiety levels allows you to manage your reactions and approach your child's unpleasant behaviors with more patience and understanding. The following chapter will explore the art of effective communication to influence your child and increase cooperation without aggression.

CHAPTER 4

Increase Cooperation With Open Communication

It is not the actions of others that trouble us, but rather, it is our own judgments. Therefore, remove those judgments and resolve to let go of your anger, and it will already be gone.

- Marcus Aurelius

Introduction to Open Communication

Open communication is the ability to share your thoughts and feelings freely while creating space for those you are communicating with to do the same. The practice of holding space in conversations allows for both the speaker and listener to feel valued despite their differences. Anything can be discussed without consequences, like being judged or criticized.

Putting open communication into practice can be challenging, especially for parents who have volatile emotions and can easily erupt when certain ideas or opinions are expressed. Sometimes, it may not be the words spoken that are triggering but the nonverbal body language of the speaker or listener.

For example, seeing your child rolling their eyes while you are conveying a message can be upsetting and cause you to derail from how you intended the conversation to go. With that said, open communication is a skill that can be learned when you are willing to listen more than you speak, seeking to understand instead of being understood, and empathizing with where your child is coming from.

For best results, it is important to teach your child and family members how to practice open communication, too. Transferring this skill will increase cooperation and help you create a family culture based on honest, transparent, and empathetic communication. In other words, your child and family members can also practice holding space for you so that you can express your hurt feelings or frustrations without feeling judged or dismissed. Furthermore, opening up to your family allows them to support you and show more understanding toward your journey of addressing your anger issues.

Here are a few communications tips to practice at home to start modeling open communication in front of your family:

- Respect the word "no," and don't force conversations or probe for answers when others seem uncomfortable.

- Show interest in others and ask questions that enable them to reflect and provide meaningful responses.

- Listen without interrupting speakers. Nod or smile while they are speaking to show that you are listening.

- Do not force apologies. Create a space where others can feel whatever they want to feel without being judged or labeled.

- Manage your expectations when it comes to the frequency of communication. Do not take offense when others choose not to communicate.

- Validate others' thoughts and feelings, regardless of whether you agree with them or not. Validation is about understanding where others are coming from and respecting their views.

How Open Communication Reduces Disagreements

One of the main benefits of open communication is how it can reduce misunderstandings and encourage both parties to find common ground. Please note that conflict cannot be completely eradicated in relationships since it is rare for people to think and feel the same all the time. However, the ability to have open discussions about minor and major issues reduces the frequency of disagreements and controls how much conflicts can grow.

When your child reaches the preteen and teenage years, it is normal for them to engage in power struggles. This refers to the practice of competing for control and questioning your leadership as a parent. Power struggles are a positive indication that your child is undergoing the process of individuation where they are becoming their own person and adopting unique ideas, beliefs, and desires about their life.

During these life stages, frequent arguments with your child can be expected. Nevertheless, these arguments don't have to be explosive. By practicing open communication skills, you can create a space for your child to say whatever is on their mind or express strong emotions without personalizing their experiences and feeling attacked. You can acknowledge that your child is their own person and has unique perspectives and preferences, which do not pose a threat to your parent-child relationship.

Of course, hearing strong words from your child is not easy, but when you look deeper and show curiosity about how they are feeling, you can empathize with their stress or pain. Behind the stubbornness or foul attitude is a human being with needs just like you. They may not express these needs like a mature person would, but that doesn't make them invalid.

Practicing healthy stress management strategies can be an effective way to prevent parent burnout and prioritize self-care. However, when stress levels become extreme, the best route is to seek professional support from a mental health specialist. If community support is something you lack, consider joining a parenting support group or contributing to parenting forums. When you share your parenting struggles with others, you realize that your symptoms are common and you are not the only mother or father struggling to cope.

EXERCISES TO ENHANCE OPEN COMMUNICATION AND COOPERATION

If you want to become a better communicator and create a safe space for your child to voice their concerns, you need to brush up on your open communication skills. The following exercises will show you how.

Exercise 25: Family Meetings

No family is the same. In some families, yelling and cursing at each other during conflict is considered normal. In other families, sweeping issues under the rug and allowing conflict to go unaddressed is normal. No matter where your family falls in this spectrum, you can all benefit from learning how to have tough conversations without hurting one another.

Family meetings are opportunities for the entire family to come together and speak about topics, events, plans, and issues that have already happened, are currently happening, or will happen soon. In this safe space, all family members have equal rights to speak and be heard. Their voices and opinions matter and are taken into consideration. Disagreements can occur during meetings, but they are handled using specific, unbiased procedures.

Not every family is ready to host family meetings. For instance, when family members do not feel safe opening up to each other, the meetings will be unproductive. Other instances where meetings will not work include:

- *One or more family members are physically or emotionally abusive.*
- *One or more family members are afraid of voicing different opinions.*
- *One or more family members feel targeted.*
- *One or more family members are not willing to listen; they dominate conversations.*
- *One or more family members do not feel like their opinions are valued.*

If your family is not yet ready to host family meetings, start by planning at least one family dinner a week where you sit together around a table and have casual discussions. Set dinner table rules to avoid breakouts of conflict. Alternatively, if you are ready to plan family meetings, use the following tips to get started:

- *Make sure all family members agree on a date and time.*
- *Keep meetings short in the beginning, between 10 and 20 minutes.*
- *Assign family members roles at the meeting (e.g., host, timekeeper, secretary, referee, etc.).*
- *Invite family members to submit conversation topics to discuss at the meeting.*
- *Read out clear communication rules that everyone must adhere to and what constitutes a family time-out (e.g., when 2 or more family members start yelling, the whole family takes a 10-minute break to cool down).*
- *Encourage all family members to contribute during meetings and speak for an equal amount of times.*
- *Reach decisions through creating problem-solving and negotiations. Write them down on a piece of paper.*

- End the meeting with a fun bonding activity that allows you to spend time together (e.g., watching a movie or comedy, going out for dinner, playing a board game, etc.).

Exercise 26: Active Listening

Good communicators are effective listeners. They can pay attention to verbal and nonverbal cues to understand the intention of a message and the perspective of the speaker. Active listening is the practice of being attentive to someone while they are speaking. This is a skill that can be developed by practicing listening and reflecting on what is shared without being quick to respond.

The magical pause after the speaker has said whatever they wanted to say allows you a few seconds or minutes to digest the message and formulate your opinion. Until then, your full focus is on listening to their words and observing their body language to collect information about what they are saying.

An active listening exercise you can play with a small child is to mime a behavior without using words. Write down a list of topics on flashcards and turn them over. Take turns picking up a card and miming the behavior using facial expressions. When the correct answer is given, it is the next person's turn. This exercise teaches young children to recognize different nonverbal cues and gestures.

For an older child, play a game of paraphrasing. Sit down on comfortable chairs and face each other. Each person gets two minutes to speak on any topic they like, and the other person must paraphrase what was said. The speaker is allowed to clarify or correct the listener if the core message was lost in translation.

Exercise 27: Nonverbal Communication

According to experts, about 70-93% of all communication is nonverbal (Ashenden, 2020). This means that the bulk of your communication lies in your body language, facial expressions, postures, and gestures. Moreover, unless your child and family members can decode your nonverbal communication, they might miss a huge component of your message.

Practicing how to read and interpret nonverbal communication with your child can significantly improve the quality of communication between you. It can also reduce the tendency to yell, curse, make threats, or become aggressive to drive specific messages. A fun game to play with older children who know how to read is wordless acting. Both of you are given a script-see below-that portrays a typical conflict scenario, which you need to act out.

Actor A will read their lines out loud, but Actor B will act out their lines without talking. Additionally, Actor B-the silent actor-will choose a secret emotional distraction from a list-see below-to influence how they act out their lines. For example, they might show signs of guilt or boredom. In the end, Actor A will need to guess what the secret emotion was that influenced Actor B's nonverbal behavior. After one round of running through the script, switch roles and choose a different secret emotion.

Script

Actor A: Hey buddy, I noticed there are still dirty dishes in the dishwasher. Have you done your chores?

Actor B: No, not yet.

Actor A: Well, why not? You know that you are supposed to do your chores before enjoying your free time.

Actor B: When I came back from school today, I had a headache and decided to sleep. I was planning on doing my chores when I woke up.

Actor A: This sounds like an excuse.

Actor B: Trust me, I'm telling the truth. Let me go and start my chores now.

List of secret emotions

- boredom
- fear
- anger
- guilt
- cheerfulness
- peace
- stress

Four Emotional Intelligence Skills

As a parent, you are emotionally invested in the well-being of your child. However, beyond desiring the best outcomes for them, it is important to understand how your behaviors and parenting approach impact their well-being. EQ is multifaceted and revolves around four core skills: self-awareness, self-regulation, social awareness, and

Exercise 28: Positive Reinforcement

Communicating with a difficult child can be challenging, especially when they are unwilling to listen. Your default response could be to raise your voice, make threats, or retaliate with harsh words. However, this only makes their behavior worse.

Positive reinforcement is a type of discipline approach that seeks to reinforce desirable behaviors by incentivizing them and punishing undesirable behaviors by withdrawing attention-pretending like you don't notice or aren't affected by your child's bad habits. After some time, your child learns that behaving well feels rewarding and misbehaving doesn't pay off.

Next are four types of positive reinforcers and examples of how you can practice them:

Natural Reinforcers

Natural reinforcers are the positive outcomes that come from positive behaviors. You don't need to plan natural reinforcers because they happen naturally. For example, when your child goes to bed earlier, the natural reinforcer is waking up feeling energized. Your job as a parent is to show your child the link between their positive behaviors and the results they can bring.

Social Reinforcers

Social reinforcers are rewards that come from social recognition. When your child behaves well, they are praised by you, their teachers, and classmates. Receiving recognition from others feels good because it promotes a sense of belonging and enables your child to see themself as worthy and competent. Here are examples of affirming words you can give your child when they do something praiseworthy:

- *Thank you for cleaning your room.*
- *You expressed your thoughts so clearly. Well done.*
- *I noticed an improvement in your math test. Keep it up!*
- *You are doing your best and I respect that.*

Tangible Reinforcers

Tangible reinforcers are physical gifts you give your child to show them how impressed you are with their behavior. These gifts do not need to be expensive to make an impact. They can be affordable and thoughtful gifts related to the positive behavior celebrated.

For example, if your child gets a good grade on their school test, you can buy them a cool set of coloring pens and a notebook that they can use to take down notes or journal.

Token Reinforcers

Token reinforcers are tangible rewards that have a nonmonetary value. They work best in a rewards system where tokens are earned for good behavior and can be exchanged for a physical gift or experience. You can use token reinforcers to reward everyday positive behaviors and encourage your child to carry out healthy habits consistently.

Exercise 29: Storytelling

The best way to explain to your child why you are the way you are or why certain values or house rules are important is to share stories about your childhood. Recall memories of when you were their age and what growing up in your household was like. Describe to your child the relationship with your parents and what you were given or not given. Compare and contrast your upbringing with theirs to help them gain a broader perspective of life.

To become a great storyteller, you need to master sequencing (i.e., intro, body, conclusion). Practice writing age-appropriate short stories-maximum 300 words each-about the following topics related to your childhood. Use sequencing to break up your stories and create a natural build-up of suspense. You can also add metaphors, analogies, and emotive language to bring your stories to life.

- *childhood family-household rules*
- *school life and relationships with teachers and peers*
- *family bonds (e.g., how close was your family?)*
- *sharing thoughts and feelings (e.g., were you encouraged to express yourself?)*
- *parental discipline (e.g., how did your parents teach you right*

from wrong?)
- future prospects (e.g., what did you want to be when you were older? How much support did you get at home?)

Exercise 30: Mindful Communication

Mindful communication is about being aware of what you are thinking and feeling and how that might impact the conversation you are having with your child. It teaches you how to regulate your emotions before and during conversations to avoid projecting your strong feelings or judgments onto your child.

For example, before going into a tough conversation, you can mentally prepare yourself by setting intentions for the desired outcomes. On a piece of paper, write down responses to the following questions:

1. How would you like to leave the conversation?
2. How would you like your child to leave the conversation?
3. What core message would you like to express? How would you like your child to feel when you express this message?
4. What actions would you like your child to take after the conversation?

During the conversation, you can practice mindful communication by recognizing when it is safe or unsafe to continue the discussion. The traffic light analogy can alert you when you have gone from a green light (i.e., open mind and heart), passed through a yellow light (i.e., triggered and on the verge of shutting down), and come to a halt at a red light (i.e., defensive and aggressive behavior).

Please note that open communication is only possible when you have an open mind and heart. However, you can turn the conversation around at a yellow light by demonstrating curiosity and empathy for your child. Once you notice that you have shut down and become defensive, it is best to conclude the conversation or postpone for a few minutes to take a parent time-out-see Chapter 2.

Exercise 31: Using Open-Ended Questions

If the lines of communication are closing or have been closed for a while between you and your child, asking open-ended questions can be a nonintrusive way to reopen them. The benefit of using open-ended questions in conversations is that they encourage your child to engage with you on a deeper level. They are prompted to think and formulate a meaningful response instead of giving quick yes or no answers. The more you get them talking, the more comfortable they will be to share their thoughts without the fear of judgment.

There are different ways to ask open-ended questions in conversations. For each example mentioned below, come up with three unique variations of your own.

Opening conversations with open-ended questions

- *Tell me about your day at school.*
- *How did you sleep last night?*
- *What are some things you dislike about our house rules?*

Seeking clarity with open-ended questions

- *Can you explain what you truly mean when you say, "Don't bother"?*
- *You mentioned that you feel misunderstood sometimes. Can you describe the last time you did it?*
- *I understand that this school transition is difficult for you. Can you give me examples of what you are struggling with?*

Turning hypothetical scenarios into open-ended questions

- *If you could give me feedback on my parenting, what would you say?*
- *If you got to choose your chores, would you feel motivated to do them?*
- *If you could ask me for anything nonphysical, what would it be?*

Exercise 32: Communication Journal

To stay connected with your child and family members, it is important to continuously check in and show interest in each other's individual lives. This allows you all to understand what each person needs, how each person feels, and any problems that need to be addressed.

A great way to create this culture in your family is to have a shared communication journal accessible to all family members. Inside this notebook, anyone can leave journal entries of different topics and lengths. The entries can be read by the whole family either at family meetings or anytime. Encourage family members to leave a blank page open after each entry so readers can also leave comments. This form of communication can be helpful for family members who find face-to-face conversations difficult.

By practicing open communication, you can learn to share your thoughts and emotions without resorting to explosive outbursts. Moreover, the skill teaches you how to connect to your child's thoughts and emotions and understand where they are coming from, even if you disagree. Still staying on the subject of open communication, the next chapter will look at different ways to resolve conflict with your child without compromising the strength of your relationship.

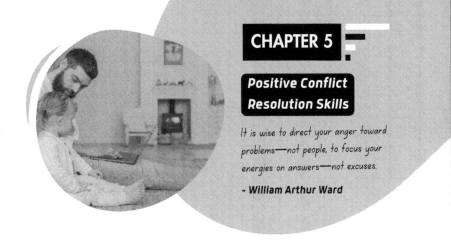

CHAPTER 5

Positive Conflict Resolution Skills

It is wise to direct your anger toward problems—not people, to focus your energies on answers—not excuses.

- **William Arthur Ward**

Introduction to Conflict Resolution

It is normal for parents and children to get into arguments over unmet expectations or troublesome behaviors. Part of children's natural process of growing up and finding their place in the world is to test boundaries. Sometimes, this could be a deliberate act of rebellion. Still, other times, it is simply their way of learning the difference between acceptable and unacceptable behavior and which consequences follow specific actions.

In traditional homes, children are raised to avoid arguments with their parents because this response is seen as a sign of disrespect. Parents take on an authoritarian style of leadership where they have complete power and decision-making ability. While this style of discipline seems to work when children are younger (i.e., most children can follow their parents' wishes without a challenge), it can lead to defiance during adolescence. Moreover, the inability of children to think for themselves and question ideas and beliefs can lead to low self-esteem, fear of independence, and failure to be individuated from their parents.

In other words, it is necessary for your child to feel confident raising concerns and having a difference of opinion, even if it means disagreeing with you as their parent. Your child's disapproval of family rules or expectations is not a sign of disrespect; instead, it is a sign of them growing up and becoming their own person. With that said, it is your responsibility as the parent to learn and teach your child conflict resolution skills so that how you both approach conflict situations improves-rather than threatens-the quality of your relationship.

The Wrong and Right Way to Discipline Difficult Children

There is a constructive and a nonconstructive way of resolving conflict with your child. The common mistake that parents make is seeking win-lose outcomes where they come out as the winner (i.e., get their children to follow orders) and their children come out as the losers (i.e., forfeit their needs and desires). The reason why parents use this approach is to assert their dominance and prevent their children from deviating from the family norms.

When these children grow up, they adopt the same unhealthy conflict resolution style of their parents and seek win-lose outcomes. For example, when their requests are denied, they are likely to engage in power struggles until, eventually their parents give in. The tables are turned, and now, it is the teenage children who seek dominance.

Win-lose outcomes mean that only parents or children can win, but never both parties. The focus during conflict resolution is for both parents and children to prove how right they are and how wrong the other person is. Both parties are defensive and struggle to listen and empathize with each other's positions.

Furthermore, walking away as the winner often means going to great lengths to defeat the opponent, which entails finding ways to exploit their weaknesses and hurt them with words or actions.

The more resilient the opponent seems, the harsher the measures to pull them down and get them to concede defeat. Many parents physically, mentally, and emotionally harm their children over petty arguments for the sake of asserting their power.

The constructive approach to conflict resolution looks and feels different. The intention of walking into these tough conversations is for both sides, parents and children, to feel seen and validated. As such, parents seek win-win outcomes so that the conversation is balanced and mutually beneficial solutions can be reached. To achieve this, parents have to be the ones who lead with an open mind and heart and seek to listen and understand where their children are coming from. This requires humility and self-awareness, recognizing the power they have and choosing to use it to empower their children rather than putting them down.

Moreover, parents practice seeing their children as individuals who have minds of their own and are capable of articulating their needs. They show respect for their children's different perspectives and hold space for them to freely share their views and justifications. Children are also given some decision-making power over certain challenges that affect their lives. Of course, parents still have the final say; however, children are consulted, and their suggestions are taken into consideration.

Learning and implementing constructive conflict resolution can teach your child healthy ways of expressing their disapproval and managing conflict. As a result, they become less afraid of disagreeing with others and advocating for their needs. Furthermore, constructive conflict resolution will show your child how to understand and negotiate with people who have different perspectives without becoming domineering. These skills will not only improve their relationships with family members within your household but also with school teachers, classmates, and future employers, too.

EXERCISES TO CULTIVATE POSITIVE CONFLICT RESOLUTION SKILLS

If you would like to learn how to resolve conflict without jeopardizing the relationship with your children, here are practical exercises that can help you learn and adopt positive conflict resolution strategies:

Exercise 33: Creative Conflict Resolution

To put a positive twist on conflict, it is important to remove the fear associated with entering disagreements. Train yourself and teach your child to view conflicts as an opportunity to solve problems and collaborate on solutions together. Look into creative ways of approaching conflict resolution that can reduce stress and create a safe environment to exchange ideas.

Here are some suggestions to consider:

- **Role-playing with puppets:** Use puppets or toys as a buffer to express strong thoughts and emotions without directly communicating with each other. You can have fun with this exercise by altering your speaking voice and showcasing your puppet's silly personality. Make sure you both get an opportunity to express your concerns and bounce back ideas on a way forward.

- **Creative writing:** For a child who dislikes confrontation, encourage them to write you a letter expressing how they feel. Read the letter and write a response that validates their emotions and seeks to find common ground. Continue writing each other letters back and forth until you come to a resolution.

- **Painting feelings:** When you don't have the words to express how you feel, you can paint them. Invite your child to join you in painting pictures of how you both may be feeling. If you don't have paint you can draw pictures using coloring pencils.

Once you are done, present your artwork to each other and explain them. Observe your child's verbal and nonverbal communication to truly understand what they may be experiencing.

- **Writing poetry or song lyrics:** Write your child a poem or a song expressing how you are feeling and encourage them to do the same. Read each other's poems and songs and try to interpret what they mean. Seek clarity to make sure you have interpreted the message correctly. Finally, collaborate on a poem or song that combines elements of your original works and highlights the way forward.

- **Brainstorming solutions:** On a piece of paper, create a mind map with the problem in the center of the page. Take turns blurting out potential solutions that come to your mind. These should be short phrases that can be written around the problem. When you have run out of ideas, look at what you have come up with and narrow the ideas down to 10, then 5, and then 3. As you narrow down your ideas, allow your child to justify why some will work or won't. Validate their reasoning and show your willingness to compromise.

Exercise 34: Communicating Boundaries

To prevent ongoing conflict, be clear with your child about what healthy and unhealthy behaviors look like, and hold them accountable for their behaviors. A simple way to do this is by communicating boundaries. We can define boundaries as healthy limits that encourage self-control. Each person has their own set of personal boundaries, and households have boundaries, too.

For example, there may be certain language you do not allow your child to use. Communicating this boundary helps your child regulate their speech. Or maybe you have certain rules about playing inside the house, helping with house chores, or hanging around friends.

Being open and transparent with your child about these rules can prevent misunderstandings and unnecessary power struggles. Additionally, boundaries create a new behavioral benchmark to hold your child accountable to. When they do not meet this benchmark, you can gently correct their behavior through appropriate consequences.

The Acknowledge, Communicate, Target (ACT) boundary-setting technique is designed to help you set healthy limits with your child in a nonaggressive and compassionate way. The aim is to show respect for your child's feelings while being clear and firm about what you expect from them. Here are the steps to practice the ACT technique:

A: Acknowledge the Feeling

Instead of criticizing your child for their mistakes, take a moment to calm yourself down and reflect on what they might have been feeling at the time. For instance, when they lost their temper, might they have been feeling overwhelmed? Or when they stayed past the curfew, might they have been enjoying their sense of freedom?
Example: "I know that you get excited to spend time with your friends because you hardly go out during the week."

C: Communicate the Problem and Set a Limit-Boundary

Now that you are both on the same page, explain why their actions could be considered harmful, irresponsible, disrespectful, or whatever the offense may be. Avoid making "You" statements that might come across as shifting blame or making judgments. Set a limit by clearly stating what you cannot accept from them.
Example: "... but returning home past your curfew goes against our agreement and cannot happen again."

T: Target an Alternative Behavior

Propose an alternative behavior to the problem you are seeking to solve. If you have an older child, be prepared for a counteroffer and negotiate until you can both agree on the best way forward. If you are dealing with a difficult child, present two choices and allow them to pick one they prefer.

Example: *"You can either honor your curfew and come back home on time, or I will have to fetch you whenever you go out."*

A complete message would sound like this: "I know that you get excited to spend time with your friends because you hardly go out during the week, but returning home past your curfew goes against our agreement and cannot happen again. You can either honor your curfew and come back home on time, or I will have to fetch you whenever you go out."

Use the same formula to create at least five different scenarios of setting and communicating boundaries.

Exercise 35: Natural vs. Logical Consequences

Boundary violations should never go unaddressed, no matter how minor you believe the bad behavior was. Remember, your child is constantly testing to see how much they can get away with it. When you overlook boundary violations, the message they get is that behaving well is optional.

Consequences are not a form of punishment. They are reminders that not every choice is the best choice to make. The aim of enforcing consequences is to teach your child how to make better choices and modify their reactions and behaviors. Therefore, effective consequences are teachable moments that cause your child to reassess their choices.

Two types of consequences lead to positive behavioral changes: natural and logical consequences. Natural consequences happen as a result of the law of cause and effect. You don't need to plan these types of consequences; they spontaneously occur on their own. For example, the natural consequence of your child not studying for a test is a low grade. If they repeat the same behavior-not studying for their tests-they will get the same disappointing results.

When you notice a pattern, you might offer a compassionate warning and suggest alternative behavior. You might say, "If you continue to put minimal preparation for your tests, you will continue to get low scores. Why not create a study timetable and start preparations at least two weeks earlier? That way, you have less pressure to cram work the day or night before the test."

Logical consequences are teachable moments created by parents. Whenever your child violates a boundary, your job is to find a meaningful way to reinforce the importance of following rules or practicing specific behaviors. The consequence should always match the offense and make your child stop and rethink their actions. For example, if your small child runs around in a store, the logical consequence would be to hold your hand or hold the trolley while you shop. If your teenage child refuses to listen when asked to put the TV volume down, the TV is switched off.

Here are a few more examples:

- *If your child refuses to share their toys with playmates = The toy is confiscated.*

- *If your child continues to neglect their chores = A few hours are cut from their social time to catch up on their chores.*

- *If your child draws or paints on furniture = They are only allowed to draw or paint in a specific room or outside.*

Complete the following table by deciding which type of consequence is the most suitable for each scenario. Whenever you choose a logical consequence, provide an example of an appropriate one:

Scenario	Natural	Logical	If logical, provide an example
Your child misuses stationery and school supplies.			
Your child steals money or other items.			
Your child tells lies about a teacher.			
Your child stays up late browsing through social media.			
Your child gets in trouble at school.			
Your child behaves poorly when hanging around certain friends.			
Your child has an attitude with everyone in the house.			

Exercise 36: Solutions-Focused Conflict Resolution

Solutions-focused conflict resolution is about focusing on the desired change you wish to see in your child rather than the troublesome behavior they continue to perform. This goes against traditional problem-solving approaches that start by defining and exploring the problem. It involves being resourceful and doing the best with what you have. For instance, it seeks to emphasize your child's strengths and encourage them to do more of what they are good at instead of adopting completely new behaviors and expectations.

The best time to use the solutions-focused approach is when you need an immediate solution to a pressing problem and don't have a lot of time or money to invest in large-scale interventions. For example, your child is struggling with their transition to a new school and you need to come up with quick solutions to make the transition more comfortable for them. There are three strategies you can use to come up with solutions:

- **Strategy 1:** Don't make unnecessary changes. Only intervene when you seek to improve the situation. If your child has come up with their own way of coping with stress or managing their behaviors, don't interfere unless their approach is destructive.

- **Strategy 2:** Identify and enhance your child's strengths. If your child possesses positive traits that could assist with modifying their behaviors, find ways to develop these traits more. For example, their natural curiosity about things could eliminate their tendency to procrastinate as long as they find mentally stimulating activities they enjoy.

- **Strategy 3:** Stop doing what doesn't work. Seek to identify and replace unhealthy behaviors immediately. You can do this by enforcing consequences for unhealthy behaviors and using

Exercise 37: Identify and Communicate Family Values

Identifying and communicating family values is a great way to unite on a shared vision of what your family stands for and the culture you reinforce at home. Unlike house rules that can feel restrictive, family values create a sense of purpose and belonging, which causes your family members to feel responsible for contributing toward living out these values. During moments of stress and conflict, family values increase family members' stress tolerance and cooperation, making it easier to solve problems and make the necessary changes.

If you don't already have family values, or if you would like to update your family values, follow these simple steps:

1. Reflect on the values you and your spouse grew up with. Make a note of the values that were effective and strengthened your families.

2. Imagine what spending time together and apart looks like for your family. For instance, how does your family spend weekdays and weekends? How do your children play or entertain themselves? How do you recharge as a couple?

3. Identify your strengths and weaknesses as a family. What is your family good at? What do you need to work on? What habits would help you get closer to one another?

4. Identify between 5 and 10 lifestyle categories that matter to your family. These should be growth areas that can help your family thrive. Examples include health, finance, education, spirituality, quality time, communication, playfulness, character-building, socializing and networking, and entertainment.

❺ Under each category, identify 3-5 values that you can work on developing. For each value, provide a definition based on your vision and understanding. Modify expectations for parents and children.

Here is a table of family values that can help you with the fifth step:

Love	Goal-driven	Nutrition	Accountability	Empowerment	Reading
Hard work	Growth mindset	Fitness	Courage	Family vacations	Equality
Teamwork	Acceptance	Open Communication	Adventure	Family mealtimes	Connection
Dedication	Respect	Self-control	Discipline	Family meetings	Empathy
Devotion	Resilience	Patience	Curiosity	Religious study	Support

Exercise 38: Create a Reward System

A reward system is a type of positive reinforcement that encourages cooperation and reduces conflict. The system is built on monetary or nonmonetary rewards obtained whenever desirable behavior is carried out frequently over a specific period. Typically, nonmonetary chart or sticker systems work for young children to reinforce good behaviors. Older children may need physical rewards to feel motivated to learn and practice good behaviors.

Examples of nonmonetary rewards include:

- extended curfew
- longer screen times
- carrying special treats for school lunch

- picking music selection on the ride to school
- having a friend come over for a play date

Examples of monetary rewards include:

- visiting a park or museum
- extra pocket money
- buying new clothes
- purchasing an electronic gadget on your child's wish list
- going out to dinner at your child's favorite restaurant

Below is a simple rewards chart that you can use at home. Customize the chart for your child, writing down tasks or behaviors they should aim to achieve regularly. At the end of the week, calculate their total score-combining scores for all tasks-and see which rewards they qualify for. Create a separate leger to determine reward types or levels based on scoring.

Tasks-Behaviors	Mon	Tues	Wed	Thurs	Fri	Total
Grand Total						

Exercise 39: Become a Master Negotiator

There will be times when your needs and expectations will clash with your child's needs and expectations. During those moments, you have two options: insisting on doing things your way or entering negotiations. Choosing the latter creates win-win outcomes that both you and your child will be comfortable with.

The art of successful negotiations with children of all ages is showing empathy. When you can step into your child's shoes and feel what they are feeling, you can suggest alternative solutions that help them achieve their goals while staying within the boundaries you have set. Most of the time, you will find that your child isn't fixed on their request but instead desires the experience the request might offer. Through open and collaborative conversations, you can work toward meeting in the middle and making sure you are both satisfied.

Here are some negotiation tactics that you can practice the next time your child approaches you with a request:

- **Encourage your child to come up with a list of pros and cons:** Train your child to look at both sides of an argument by weighing the pros and cons of their request. This helps them reflect on the impact of their request and why Mom or Dad might be opposed to it. They also get a second opportunity to edit their request and present something more realistic.

- **Avoid saying no to requests:** To prevent your child from being afraid to make requests, avoid rejecting them. Find other ways to help your child get what they want, even if it means starting by fulfilling your request. For example, if your child asks to visit a friend over the weekend, you can agree, provided they wash the car before they leave. If your child asks for money, you can find ways to help them earn it.

- **Link privileges to good behavior:** Teach your child that privileges must be earned through consistent, good behaviors. Whenever they make a request, encourage them to think about recent good behavior that would qualify them for the privilege. For example, going to bed on time during the week can be a good enough reason to allow your child to stay up late on Friday and Saturday.

Exercise 40: Conflict Management Style Quiz

To determine whether you are getting better at managing conflict at home, complete the conflict management style quiz regularly. According to the Thomas Kilmann Conflict Mode Instrument (TKI), there are five approaches to managing conflict: competing, collaborating, avoiding, accommodating, and compromising (Benoliel, 2017). Go through the quiz, then total your scores to see which style resonates with you.

Instruction: For each question, circle the letter that best describes the actions you take.

1. When talking to my child

- **A** I go down to their level and look at them in their eyes.
- **B** I make sure they are looking at me in the eyes.
- **C** I try to make it quick to save both of our time.
- **D** I try to make it quick to not waste their time.
- **E** I try to make the exchange mutually beneficial.

2. If my child is unhappy about a decision I have made

- **A** I arrange a time to sit down with them and hear their concerns.
- **B** I seek to highlight the value of the decision and win them over.
- **C** I allow them some time to process and adjust to the decision.
- **D** I listen to their concerns and adjust the decision accordingly.

E I listen to their concerns and look for a mutually beneficial solution.

3. When my child upsets me, I

A Call them aside and share my thoughts and feelings.

B Take away privileges to make them feel the hurt I feel.

C Go no-contact until I feel ready to confront them.

D Brush it off and move on as quickly as possible.

E Seek to explain my side of the story and give them a chance to explain theirs.

4. When my child explains a problem they are facing to me

A I get excited and try to help them the best I can.

B I try to explain that everybody experiences problems and they will be fine.

C I get irritated and ask them to go and speak to my partner.

D I allow them to vent and validate their feelings.

E I help them see their problem from different perspectives.

5. When I want to get a point across to my child without any luck

A I stop speaking and start listening.

B I speak louder and become more impatient.

C I withdraw from the conversation.

D I shut down and simply agree with whatever they are saying.

E I slow down the conversation and encourage both of us to take turns speaking and listening.

6 When I fail to deliver on a promise to my child

- **A** I apologize and explain my mistake.
- **B** I don't take it too seriously.
- **C** I pretend nothing happened.
- **D** I go above and beyond to make it up to them.
- **E** I ask them how I can make it up to them.

7 When my child violates a boundary

- **A** I sit down with them and go over the rules and expectations.
- **B** I hand out appropriate consequences immediately.
- **C** I let my partner handle the discipline.
- **D** I adjust the expectations to accommodate their needs.
- **E** I seek to understand where they are coming from, then remind them of the consequences that will follow next time.

Results

Mostly As: *Collaborative.* You are assertive and cooperative when resolving conflict.

Mostly Bs: *Competing.* You are assertive but uncooperative when resolving conflict.

Mostly Cs: *Avoiding.* You are both unassertive and uncooperative when dealing with conflict.

Mostly Ds: *Accommodating.* You sacrifice your needs and expectations to satisfy others when resolving conflict.

Mostly Es: *Compromising.* You aim to reach mutually beneficial solutions when resolving conflict.

By adopting positive conflict resolution approaches, you can create a safe space to disagree with your child without escalating your conflicts and ensure they feel comfortable engaging in tough conversations with you.

CONCLUSION

Take Control of Your Anger, One Day at a Time

Anger is an acid that can do more harm to the vessel in which it is stored than to anything on which it is poured.
- Mark Twain

Feeling angry is not an emotion you have to avoid at all costs. There are times when your anger can be useful, particularly when you are advocating for your needs, protecting your family, or expressing disappointment about your child's poor choice of behavior. You have every right to feel angry when you are upset, stressed, or overwhelmed. Nevertheless, how you express anger is a choice that you are in control of.

This comprehensive anger management workbook has provided you with 40 exercises that can help you address your anger issues and improve your parent-child relationship. For best results, practice these exercises regularly, focusing on the areas where you need extra support. You can practice the exercises alone while staring into a mirror, with your spouse, or, if you feel confident enough, with your child.

The exercises provided in this workbook cannot erase the root causes of your anger issues. However, they offer you a fresh start you can build upon alongside professional therapy. Remember that there are different kinds of resources and support available to treat anger issues. If you are interested in exploring this topic in-depth, you can purchase the full-length book that accompanies this workbook titled *The Effective Anger Management Guide for Parents: Discover How to Manage and Calm Your Emotions; Turn Your Frustration Into Positive parenting.*

ABOUT THE AUTHOR
Richard Bass

Richard Bass is a well-established author with extensive knowledge and background on children's disabilities. Richard has also experienced first-hand many children and teens who deal with depression and anxiety. He enjoys researching techniques and ideas to better serve students, as well as guiding parents on how to understand and lead their children to success.

Richard wants to share his experience, research, and practices through his writing, as it has proven successful for many parents and students.

Richard feels there is a need for parents and others around the child to fully understand the disability or the mental health of the child. He hopes that with his writing, people will be more understanding of children going through these issues.

Richard Bass has been in education for over a decade and holds a bachelor's and master's degree in education as well as several certifications, including Special Education K-12 and Educational Administration.

Whenever Richard is not working, reading, or writing, he likes to travel with his family to learn about different cultures as well as get ideas from all around about the upbringing of children, especially those with disabilities. Richard also researches and learns about different educational systems around the world.

Richard participates in several online groups where parents, educators, doctors, and psychologists share their success with children with disabilities. Richard is in the process of growing a Facebook group where further discussion about his books and techniques could take place. Apart from online groups, he has also attended trainings regarding the upbringing of students with disabilities and has also led trainings in this area.

REFERENCES

About anger. (n.d.). Mind. https://www.mind.org.uk/information-support/types-of-mental-health-problems/anger/about-anger/

Adley, L. (2021, May 18). Parent-Child conflicts: Resolution options. PACEs Connection. https://www.pacesconnection.com/g/Parenting-with-ACEs/blog/parent-child-conflicts-resolution-options

Adriane. (2020, February 22). *How to define and discover your family values*. Raising Kids with Purpose. https://raisingkidswithpurpose.com/defining-family-values/

Alder, S. L. (n.d.). *Shannon L. Alder quotes*. Goodreads. https://www.goodreads.com/author/show/1391130.Shannon_L_Alder

Alpert, A. (2022, October 19). *Six easy ways to practice gratitude as a parent*. Motherly. https://www.mother.ly/health-wellness/mental-health/how-to-practice-gratitude-as-a-parent/

Amatullah, A. (2021, November 19). *Solution-Focused approach to coaching: Questions, interventions, techniques [and example session]*. Universal Coach Institute. https://www.universalcoachinstitute.com/solution-focused/

Anger diary and triggers. (2019, March 19). MentalHelp. https://www.mentalhelp.net/anger/diary-and-triggers/#:-:text=An%20anger%20diary%20or%20journal

Ashenden, P. (2020, February 18). Nonverbal communication: How body language and nonverbal cues are key. Lifesize. https://www.lifesize.com/blog/speaking-without-words/#:-:text=However%2C%20most%20experts%20agree%20that

Astray, T. (2020, February 24). *Communication tools: Using "I-statements" when making requests in relationships.* Tatiana Astray. https://www.tatianaastray.com/managing-relationships/2020/2/10/communication-tool-using-i-statements-to-make-requests-in-relationships

Aurelius, M. (2023, April 4). *50 best anger management quotes to keep calm.* Kidadl. https://kidadl.com/quotes/best-anger-management-quotes-to-keep-calm

Barone, P. (2015, November 9). *What is role reversal?* Michigan Psychodrama Center. https://www.michiganpsychodramacenter.com/what-is-role-reversal/

Bedortha, A., Davis, C., Swartz, L., & Thompson, J. (2020, August 28). *Natural versus logical consequences.* Parenting Now. https://parentingnow.org/natural-versus-logical-consequences/#:-:text=Natural%20consequences%20are%20never%20OK%20if%20it%20puts%20your%20child%20in%20danger.&text=Logical%20consequences%20don

Benoliel, B. (2017, May 30). *What's your conflict management style?* Walden University. https://www.waldenu.edu/news-and-events/walden-news/2017/0530-whats-your-conflict-management-style

Bloudoff-Indelicato, M. (2016, March 3). *The 14 questions you should ask a therapist before your first appointment.* Washingtonian. https://www.washingtonian.com/2016/03/03/the-14-questions-you-must-ask-a-therapist-before-your-first-appointment/

BrightChamps. (2023, June 30). Teaching conflict resolution skills for kids: A parent's guide. BrightChamps Blog. https://brightchamps.com/blog/conflict-resolution-skills-for-kids/

Brodsky, S. (2022, September 15). 25 journal prompts for when you're feeling angry. Wondermind. https://www.wondermind.com/article/anger-journal-prompts/

Buddha. (2019, November 4). Anger management quotes. CompassionPower. https://compassionpower.com/anger-management-quotes/

Celebrating a child's success: Why it matters. (2023, September 5). Orchids International School. https://www.orchidsinternationalschool.com/blog/parents-corner/celebrate-a-childs-success

Chahal, G. (2022, November 24). *Practice breathing exercise to become A better parent*. LinkedIn. https://www.linkedin.com/pulse/practice-breathing-exercise-become-better-parent-guineet-chahal/

Chapman, S. G. (2010, November 23). *Stop, wait, go*. Mindful. https://www.mindful.org/stop-wait-go/

Cherney, K. (2020, November 4). *Therapy for anger: What works & who to work with*. Healthline. https://www.healthline.com/health/therapy-for-anger#how-therapy-helps

Cooks-Campbell, A. (2023, November 28). *Triggers: Learn to recognize and deal with them*. BetterUp. https://www.betterup.com/blog/triggers

Davis, T. (2022). Stress management: Definition, techniques, and strategies. The Berkeley Well-Being Institute. https://www.berkeleywellbeing.com/stress-management.html

Des Marais, S. (2019, November 21). 6 positive reinforcement examples. Psych Central. https://psychcentral.com/health/positive-reinforcement-examples

Dunlea, A. (n.d.). Grateful parenting. Grateful. https://grateful.org/resource/grateful-parenting/

Elyse. (2019, March 7). Effective conflict resolution activities for classrooms. Proud to Be Primary. https://proudtobeprimary.com/conflict-resolution-activities/

Emerson, R. W. (2019, November 4). Anger management quotes. CompassionPower. https://compassionpower.com/anger-management-quotes/

Fetsch, R. J., & Jacobson, B. (n.d.). *Ten tips for successful family meetings*. Colorado State University. https://extension.colostate.edu/topic-areas/family-home-consumer/10-tips-for-successful-family-meetings/#:-:text=The%20purpose%20of%20a%20family

Fleming, G. (2019, July 11). *4 helpful nonverbal communication activities*. ThoughtCo. https://www.thoughtco.com/nonverbal-communication-activities-1857230

Gawlik, K., & Melnyk, B. M., (2022, May). *Examining the epidemic of working parental burnout and strategies to help*. The Ohio State University. https://wellness.osu.edu/sites/default/files/documents/2022/05/OCWO_ParentalBurnout_3674200_Report_FINAL.pdf

Gibbons, S. (2018, January 14). Empathy mapping: The first step in design thinking. Nielsen Norman Group. https://www.nngroup.com/articles/empathy-mapping/

Gillespie, B. (n.d.). Self-Compassion break script from Bob Gillespie. https://www.fammed.wisc.edu/files/webfm-uploads/documents/research/stream/sc-break-script.pdf

Gottman, J. (2018, August 8). Emotional intelligence creates loving and supportive parenting. The Gottman Institute. https://www.gottman.com/blog/emotional-intelligence-creates-loving-supportive-parenting/

Hannay, C. (2019, June 14). Mindful speech: What type of conversation do you want? Mindful Teachers. https://www.mindfulteachers.org/blog/what-type-of-conversation-do-you-want

He, G. (2023, February 10). Sixteen active listening activities for the workplace. Team Building. https://teambuilding.com/blog/active-listening-activities

Hooven, C., Gottman, J. M., & Katz, L. F. (1995). Parental meta-emotion structure predicts family and child outcomes. *Cognition & Emotion*, *9*(2-3), 229-264. https://doi.org/10.1080/02699939508409010

How parents can add self-care to their daily routine. (n.d.). Smart Sitting. https://smartsitting.com/blog/how-parents-can-add-self-care-to-their-daily-routine

How to reduce stress. (n.d.). UNICEF. https://www.unicef.org/parenting/mental-health/how-reduce-stress-parents

Irritable and overwhelmed? Signs of parental burnout. (2022, July 21). CHADD. https://chadd.org/adhd-weekly/irritable-and-overwhelmed-signs-of-parental-burnout/

Jenny. (2023, November 21). *Time management hacks for working parents*. The Gingerbread House. https://the-gingerbread-house.co.uk/time-management-hacks-for-working-parents/

Kulik, D. (2022, May 13). *Parenting and conflict resolution strategies*. Dr. Dina Kulik. https://drdina.ca/parenting-and-conflict-resolution-strategies/

Lagioia, V. (2021, March). *How to help parents find the right parenting support for them*. Emerging Minds. https://emergingminds.com.au/resources/how-to-help-parents-find-the-right-parenting-support-for-them/#what-is-this-resource-about

Li, P. (2023, October 22). *Angry parents and what can you do*. Parenting for Brain. https://www.parentingforbrain.com/angry-parents/#do

Linehan, M. (n.d.). *Opposite action skill*. Dialectical Behavior Therapy (DBT) Tools. https://dbt.tools/emotional_regulation/opposite-action.php

Loggenberg, E. (n.d.). *Benefits of asking young kids open-ended questions*. Under5s. https://www.under5s.co.nz/shop/Hot+Topics+Articles/Child+Development/Benefits+of+asking+young+kids+open-ended+questions.html#:-:text=After%20asking%20your%20child%20an

Lorandini, J. (2019, April 16). *Opposite action for overwhelming emotions: How to make it work for you*. Suffolk DBT. https://suffolkdbtjl.com/opposite-action/

Managing morning routines. (n.d.). Help Me to Parent. https://helpme2parent.ie/articles/remove-stress-from-morning-routines/

Medeiros, M. (2018, May 29). 25 actually doable hobbies for stay-at-home parents. SheKnows. https://www.sheknows.com/parenting/articles/1007717/25-hobbies-for-the-stay-at-home-mom/

Meditation for stress: A guide to clear the mind. (2023, June 29). Calm Blog. https://www.calm.com/blog/meditation-for-stress

Neff, K. (2019). Definition and three elements of self compassion. Self-Compassion. https://self-compassion.org/the-three-elements-of-self-compassion-2/

Novotney, A. (2019, May). The risks of social isolation. American Psychological Association. https://www.apa.org/monitor/2019/05/ce-corner-isolation#:-:text=%22Lacking%20encouragement%20from%20family%20or

Pangaro, K. (2021, June 22). 9 time management hacks for the busy parent. Atomic Mommy. https://atomicmommy.net/2021/06/22/time-management-hacks/

Quinn, A., Kemp, C. J., & Fruhauf, C. A. (n.d.). *Dealing with couples' anger*. Colorado State University. https://extension.colostate.edu/topic-areas/family-home-consumer/dealing-with-couples-anger-10-238/

Robboy, A. C. (n.d.). *Identifying your triggers with a PTSD trigger table*. The Center for Growth. https://www.thecenterforgrowth.com/tips/identifying-your-triggers-with-a-ptsd-trigger-table

Robinson, A. (2017, October 27). Three steps for setting boundaries. Amanda Robinson LPC. https://amandarobinsonlpc.com/2017/10/27/3-steps-for-setting-boundaries/

Russell, L. (2023, July 17). *The essential parent's tool: Our free anger thermometer*. They Are the Future. https://www.theyarethefuture.co.uk/anger-thermometer/#:-:text=An%20anger%20thermometer%20is%20a

Stanborough, R. J. (2020, February 4). *Cognitive restructuring: Techniques and examples*. Healthline. https://www.healthline.com/health/cognitive-restructuring#how-does-it-work

The benefits of and techniques for managing stress. (2018, October 31). Houston Behavioral Health. https://www.houstonbehavioralhealth.com/blog/techniques-for-managing-stress

Tillotson, K. (2023, December 17). *A parent's guide to the four pillars of emotional intelligence*. Self Help Books for Kids. https://selfhelpbooksforkids.com/a-parents-guide-to-the-four-pillars-of-emotional-intelligence/

Trotman, W. G. (n.d.). *Wayne Gerard Trotman quotes*. Goodreads. https://www.goodreads.com/author/show/4593149.Wayne_Gerard_Trotman

Twain, M. (2023, April 4). *50 best anger management quotes to keep calm*. Kidadl. https://kidadl.com/quotes/best-anger-management-quotes-to-keep-calm

Twenty-nine ways to celebrate and reward your child's achievements. (2021, January 6). BritMums. https://www.britmums.com/29-ways-to-celebrate-your-childs-achievements/

Ward, W. A. (2023, April 4). *50 best anger management quotes to keep calm*. Kidadl. https://kidadl.com/quotes/best-anger-management-quotes-to-keep-calm

What is emotional intelligence and how does it apply to the workplace? (2023). Mental Health America. https://mhanational.org/what-emotional-intelligence-and-how-does-it-apply-workplace

Why children crave consistency and clear expectations. (n.d.). First5California. https://www.first5california.com/en-us/articles/why-children-crave-consistency-and-clear-expectations/

Yeh, K. (2020, December 27). Self-Care 101 for parents: 6 ways to kickstart your self-care routine. My Self-Love Supply. https://myselflovesupply.com/blogs/blog/self-care-101-for-parents-6-ways-to-kickstart-your-self-care-routine

Your Zen Mama. (2020, December 11). How to teach your children the art of negotiation. Your Zen Mama. https://www.yourzenmama.com/new-blog/how-to-teach-your-children-the-art-of-negotiation

IMAGE REFERENCES

Burton, K. (2021). Tired mother with black boy [Image]. Pexels. https://www.pexels.com/photo/tired-mother-with-black-boy-6624312/

Danilyuk, P. (2021). A child sitting beside his working father [Image]. Pexels. https://www.pexels.com/photo/a-child-sitting-beside-his-working-father-7220966/

de Richelieu, A. (2020). Father looking at his son playing on a smartphone [Image]. Pexels. https://www.pexels.com/photo/father-looking-at-his-son-playing-on-a-smartphone-4260640/

Fring, G. (2020). Mother going crazy with small children at home [Image]. Pexels. https://www.pexels.com/photo/mother-going-crazy-with-small-children-at-home-4017408/

Green, A. (2020). Woman in desperate and anxiety sitting alone [Image]. Pexels. https://www.pexels.com/photo/woman-in-desperate-and-anxiety-sitting-alone-5699860/

Nilov, M. (2021). Food man person couple [Image]. Pexels. https://www.pexels.com/photo/food-man-person-couple-6933132/

Subiyanto, K. (2020). Happy mother and children hugging at home [Image]. Pexels. https://www.pexels.com/photo/happy-mother-and-children-hugging-at-home-4474043/

Printed in Great Britain
by Amazon